Ian Allan abc LONDON UNDERGROUND

JOHN GLOVER

IAN ALLAN
Publishing

First published 1997

ISBN 0 7110 2545 2

Published by Ian Allan Publishing

an imprint of Ian Allan Ltd, Terminal House, Station Approach, Shepperton, Surrey TW17 8AS.
Printed by Ian Allan Printing Ltd at its works at Coombelands in Runnymede, England.

Code: 9711/C2

Front cover:
An Uxbridge-bound train arrives at Ruislip on 15 March 1997.

Back cover:
Central Line 1992 stock (left) and Jubilee Line 1996 stock (right) stand side-by-side at Ruislip depot on 15 March 1997.

Previous page:
Four parallel tracks are uncommon on the Underground. Here, a southbound A stock train on the Metropolitan main line overtakes a 1983 stock Jubilee Line train as it prepares to stop at West Hampstead.

Picture credits
All photographs are by the author unless otherwise credited.

Acknowledgements
There are many people who, in one way or another, have assisted in the compilation of this book. I am grateful to them all, but it would be invidious to name some and inadvertently omit others. However, the conclusions are my own, and they do not purport to represent the views of London Regional Transport or London Underground Ltd.

Contents

INTRODUCTION

London Underground has been with us for a long time, to the extent that it now requires what the corporate image makers recently described as a '1,000 billion mile service'. In this, the system reflects both the difficulties of the pioneer, and the cumulative lack of attention which has been afforded to politically unexciting matters such as the upkeep of the infrastructure and track renewals over past decades.

The purpose of this book is to provide in a single volume a concise overview of London Underground, the half-twilight world of mass transit. It is, perhaps, an appropriate time to take stock.

The scene is set by the historical context, under which the various lines were built by private enterprise with little attempt at control by public bodies. Later, public moneys became available, but initially this was as much

Possible extensions to existing lines or altogether new lines are always a topic for discussion, and the prospects for the major schemes are examined. But journeys are rarely taken for their own sake, and the future of the Underground is bound up with the type of city which London hopes to be in the future.

The story will continue to evolve. However, as London Underground heads for record levels of both traffic and service provision, a secure base from which to breach the £1 billion a year sales revenue milestone will be essential.

And London Underground looks rather wider than just at its passengers:

'In London Underground, we see all those who benefit from our services as our customers, not just those who  travel on our services. Our purpose is to achieve the best possible service for all. As well as fare paying customers, this therefore includes business interests, the London community and Government, who buy wider benefits such as reduced road traffic and better air quality on behalf of London'. (Memorandum to Select Committee on Transport, 19 February 1997.)

to relieve unemployment as to weld together the transport system the capital city needed.

Consideration is then afforded to the present organisational arrangements, in which London Underground is a subsidiary company of London Regional Transport, and the responsibilities of each body. This is followed by a review of the sources of Underground traffic and where the strengths and weaknesses lie.

There is a description of the Underground on a line-by-line basis and of the surface and tube stock trains which provide the service. This leads to a discussion of where the Underground is today.

The Underground does not exist in a vacuum, and the involvement of outside bodies is examined briefly.

Above:
A 1992 stock train built by ADtranz for the Central Line approaches North Acton Junction with an eastbound train from West Ruislip in July 1994. This forms part of the route of the longest through journey on London Underground, from West Ruislip to Epping.

Opposite:
Welcome to the Underground. The bright and cheery St John's Wood Jubilee Line station, opened in 1939, may be fraying at the edges, but it still carries all the attributes of good design.

1
SYSTEM DEVELOPMENT

The First Underground Railways

London is a port, its original situation determined primarily by the availability of drinking water and the ability to construct quays. It was founded by the Romans in about AD50. Superior drainage on the north bank led to this developing first. By 1700, London was the world's leading business centre. The Thames was an extremely convenient highway and travel by boat was the cheapest form of transport.

Between 1811 and 1871 the population trebled, from 1.3 million to 3.8 million, to become the world's largest city. Central London was dominated by the hansom cab and then the horse bus; traffic congestion was serious. This was not helped by the exclusion of the mainline railways from central London, which were forced to terminate on the outskirts along what is now the line of the Euston Road, or south of the Thames. Although this requirement was later relaxed, notably in the cases of Charing Cross, Victoria and Cannon Street, the results are with us still.

The answer was to go underground, and the first part of the Metropolitan Railway between Paddington and Farringdon was opened in 1863. The line was built in the main by the cut-and-cover method whereby a trench is dug, tracks laid and the whole is then roofed over. This method had obvious and very public shortcomings during the construction phase. The Metropolitan was an immediate success, and by the following year 12 million passenger journeys were being made upon its modest 5.91km. The line's purpose was to link the Great Western Railway's Paddington terminus with the City, and the railway managed to serve Euston and King's Cross at the same time. The diagram shows the extent of the Underground system by 1933.

The Metropolitan was followed by the Metropolitan District Railway, the genesis of today's District Line. Both expanded their route networks, but the companies were 'no relation' as they say, and acted accordingly. With some parliamentary prodding, the companies eventually completed what is today's Circle Line in 1884.

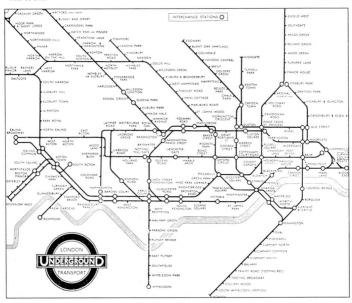

4

Left: The façade of Paddington Praed Street Metropolitan Railway station dates from 1868. No Metropolitan trains have served it for years. Presently, this is the entrance for Circle and District Line services, although the Bakerloo can also be reached.

Expansion outwards took the Metropolitan to Amersham (1892) and beyond, and the District to Richmond (1877), Ealing Broadway (1879), Hounslow West (1884, now part of the Piccadilly), and Wimbledon (1889). Some of this was achieved by joint running over the tracks of the main line railways. Eastwards, Whitechapel was reached in 1884, and with it today's East London Line. The tunnel under the Thames had been bored by the Brunels, father and son, and completed as a pedestrian walkway in 1843. It was extended at each end and converted for railway use in 1869 and was first used by the Underground in 1884.

The surface lines comprise the Metropolitan, the Hammersmith & City, the Circle, the District and the East London. Most of the in-town sections are built directly below present-day roads.

Initially, steam traction was used, with conversion to electricity in the first few years of the 20th century. One lasting benefit arising from the cut-and-cover construction method was the shallow depth of the station platforms. Typically, these are only about 7m below ground level. Consequently, access by stairs was sufficient, at least during the Victorian era.

The tunnels are of relatively large cross-section, approaching the dimensions used on National Railways. The trains used are noticeably larger, particularly in height, than those on the tube lines.

Left: The Underground as it was in 1933. *Author's collection*

Below: Farringdon station moved to its present site in 1865; an A stock train is seen arriving with a service for Aldgate. The platforms on the left are for the Widened Lines services, now known as Thameslink and electrified at 25kV ac at this point as well as a dc third rail.

Above: The northbound platform at the former City & South London station at Euston was filled in to allow cross-platform interchange to the Victoria Line. A southbound 1972 MkII Northern Line train arrives. The platform surfacing has not succeeded in hiding the join; the photographer would have been balancing on his right leg had the widening not taken place.

The Tube Lines

The surface lines clearly had their disadvantages, which included the inability to pass beneath watercourses which were not suitable to be piped. This need was to be met by the construction of the deep level tube railway. The development of the tubes required relative perfection in three technical areas:

- the method of boring tunnels in the London clay as a means of construction;
- the successful development of the use of electricity for traction purposes; and
- the use of the lift, largely replaced later by the escalator, to gain access to deep level platforms at an average 25m below ground level.

Other matters to be addressed concerned ventilation and drainage. The above conditions were satisfied by the time of the inauguration of the 5.2km City & South London Railway from King William Street (in the City) to Stockwell in 1890 and the Waterloo & City in 1898. By the time of World War 1, much of today's tube infrastructure in central London was in place. London's population had continued to grow, reaching 7.1 million by 1911.

Above left: Tooting Bec was one of the stations in the southern extension of the City & South London Railway to Morden, which was opened in 1926. Originally named Trinity Road (Tooting Bec), the station has been restored to near original condition at street level in recent times.

Above right: A 1973 stock train is about to leave the open air as it approaches Southgate Piccadilly Line station on a southbound journey. Southgate was a 1933 creation.

System Growth

The Underground network as we know it today was built over a number of distinct periods. The years 1863-99 saw the major building of the surface lines and their extensions, and the very start of tube construction. The period thence to 1918 saw the virtual completion of the surface network, with Upminster (District) reached in 1902, Uxbridge (Metropolitan) in 1904 and Ealing Common-Rayners Lane (then District, now Piccadilly) in

1910. Frenetic tube building saw the opening of the central parts of today's Bakerloo, Central, Northern and Piccadilly lines, and a good bit more, seeing that all had to locate and then reach a depot site on the surface. By 1913, the tube ran between Liverpool Street and Wood Lane Shepherd's Bush (Central), Elephant & Castle and Paddington (Bakerloo), Finsbury Park and Hammersmith (Piccadilly), Charing Cross and Archway/Golders Green, also Clapham Common and Euston via Bank (Northern).

Construction of the Underground, by period of time

Route Km	1863-99	1900-18	1919-34	1935-49	1950-98	Totals	%
East London	6.18	1.04				7.22	1.7
Metropolitan	62.51	16.67	3.31			82.49	19.6
District	44.13	32.75		1.01		77.89	18.5
Total, surface	106.64	49.42	3.31	1.01	0.00	160.38	38.2
%	66	31	2	1	0	100	
Bakerloo		23.55				23.55	5.6
Central		9.87	7.70	54.98		72.55	17.3
Jubilee			7.24	10.84	21.62	39.70	9.5
Northern	3.93	20.34	20.29	13.61		58.17	13.8
Piccadilly		14.17	16.70		11.19	42.06	10.0
Victoria					21.28	21.28	5.1
Waterloo & City	2.37					2.37	0.6
Total, tube	6.30	67.93	51.93	79.43	54.09	259.68	61.8
%	2	26	20	31	21	100	
All lines	112.94	117.35	55.24	80.44	54.09	420.06	100
%	27	28	13	19	13	100	
Period (years)	37	19	16	15	49	136	
Rte km/year	3.05	6.18	3.45	5.36	1.10	3.09	

The Underground pushed into the developing suburbs in the 1919-34 period, during which Ealing Broadway was reached by the Central Line in 1920, Watford (Metropolitan) in 1925, Stanmore (then Metropolitan, now Jubilee) in 1932 and Cockfosters (Piccadilly) in 1933. A major reconstruction of the City & South London Railway and its linking with the Charing Cross, Euston & Hampstead, with extensions to both Morden and Edgware, was completed in 1926. This is most of the present Northern Line.

Such works were assisted by the Trade Facilities Act of 1921, whereby the Government provided a Treasury guarantee or new works capital. The aim then, and subsequently, was to encourage capital schemes which were fully justified in terms of demand but, crucially, to reduce unemployment. It was in a period during which Lord Ashfield, Chairman of the Underground Group and later the London Passenger Transport Board remarked:

'It may be a great surprise to you to know that the Underground railways in London have never been, in their whole career, a financial success. In other words, they have failed to earn anything approaching a reasonable return on capital invested in them, notwithstanding the fact that they have been able to select the most advantageous routes'.

Piccadilly trains were extended west from Hammersmith in 1932/3, on new construction as far as Acton Town and then over tracks later vacated by the District.

This era was followed by the 1935-40 New Works Programme, which was a mix of new construction and the assimilation of unwanted parts of the mainline railways. Separate tracks were completed for today's Jubilee Line between Baker Street and Wembley Park in 1939. High Barnet (1940) and Mill Hill East (1941) became Northern Line outposts, while completion of the Central Line extensions to West Ruislip (1948) and Epping (1949) had to await the end of World War 2 hostilities.

London's population reached a peak of 8.1 million in 1939, since when it has fallen gently to around seven million today. The 1950s were a prolonged standstill period for the Underground. It was not until 1963 that the first stage of the Victoria Line, long campaigned for, received the go-ahead. The Victoria Line was opened in stages from 1968 to 1972. 1975 saw the loss of the Moorgate-Finsbury Park line, once owned by the Metropolitan, to British Rail's Great Northern suburban services. These were then in process of electrification.

The Piccadilly reached Heathrow Central (original name) in 1977 and the loop via Terminal 4 was completed in 1986. The Jubilee Line was opened to Charing Cross (1979) with new construction from Baker Street southwards, and the extension from Green Park to Stratford is due to open in 1998.

This necessarily brief tour of the growth of the Underground system is illustrated in the table on the previous page.

The table indicates that well over half the system had been built by 1918, and that later construction was almost all on the tube lines. It also shows the relative lack of progress in the last half century. In terms of length of the system as built, the tube accounted for 60%, though transfers from the surface lines as explained above have now increased that proportion slightly.

It should be noted that all lines are classified in accordance with their original construction. Thus, the Wembley Park-Stanmore line is shown under the Metropolitan which built it, rather than as part of the Jubilee. Likewise, the Piccadilly's present western branches appear under the District. The table includes only those lines which are open today; those on which passenger services were later completely withdrawn have been excluded. It is hoped that readers will forgive this simplified approach, which is intended to show clearly the main periods of activity at the expense of detail.

Gaps in the System

London Underground runs primarily north of the Thames, with only 33 stations (including those on the Jubilee Line Extension) south of the river out of the total of 273 stations served.

Although the Romans built on both sides of the

Borough	No of LUL stations	% residents travelling to work by LUL
City of Westminster	28	24-29
Brent	20	24-29
Camden	19	24-29
Hammersmith & Fulham	14	30-35
Ealing	14	18-23
Barnet	13	18-23

Thames, the central core was on the north bank, where it has remained. In their time, the river was 300m across, compared with about 100m today. At high tide, it would be 1,000m wide, with shallow water covering Southwark. The combination of wet conditions and sands and gravels replacing the London clay, which was ideal for tunnelling, combined to make the south bank unattractive for Underground railway construction.

Another reason was the influence of the mainline railways. While those running to the north of England had more important and profitable traffics on their mind than local passenger operations, the southern companies had effectively no industrial base. What became suburban traffic was thus fought over jealously and closely guarded; it was made very clear to the Underground that intrusion would not be welcomed.

Which parts of London have the most Underground stations? The table on page 8 shows the top six boroughs, and 1991 journey to work census data.

In each case, the proportion travelling by National Railways is 5% or less. Progressing further down the list, the situation of course changes. Residents of the boroughs in southeast London show a corresponding affinity with National Railways, and have little interest in LUL.

Below: **The present Jubilee Line was opened in 1979 to Charing Cross. A southbound train of 1983 stock arrives at Bond Street.**

The System Itself

The Underground system, despite its long-standing name, is mostly above ground. The proportions of route length, by construction type, are as follows:

sub-surface cut and cove	8%
deep level tube	36%
lines on the surface	56%
total	**100%**

In this context, 'surface' does not imply at grade. Rather, Underground lines may be carried on embankments, bridging or viaducts, in cuttings or between retaining walls.

Similarly, what may be called a tunnel will vary considerably in methods of construction. Tunnels may be classified as:

cast iron	206km
concrete	33km
brick	25km
covered way	103km

Within this group, cast iron is the traditional lining in bored tube tunnel construction, replaced in more recent times with concrete segments. Having said that, the earliest tunnels, as on the East London Line, are of brick. The covered way is mostly the cut-and-cover construction of the surface lines in the central area.

Tube and Surface

The history of the Underground shows that surface trains were in existence about a quarter of a century before the tubes; as a result, there are two systems which have considerable technical differences. They do share a track gauge of 1,435mm and a traction voltage of 630V dc. Inter-running is possible, but there are considerable constraints. Not the least of these is the differing height of the floors of tube cars and surface cars above rail level. With tube cars this is 610mm, surface cars 980mm.

The development by line extension of the surface system all but ceased with the Metropolitan Watford branch construction, whereas the tube system continues to expand today.

A principal reason was the size of the running tunnels. With a bored tunnel, the diameter rises from around 3,700mm to perhaps 4,900mm. As a consequence, the volume of spoil to be removed increases by around 80%. The tunnel lining requirements also increase by a third, and the whole is ever more difficult to fit into the space available. Similar calculations apply whether the tunnels are bored or of cut-and-cover construction.

The net effect is that construction costs of approaching double that for tube lines are incurred by surface lines. In the era discussed, such extravagance (as it may have seemed) would not have been conducive to obtaining a decision to proceed.

Sadly, though, the gains from large bore construction are not great. Measured in terms of floor space, the surface stock gives at most a 10% increase in car width. There is a gain in headroom and a surface car is probably a more comfortable vehicle in which to stand if necessary, but the capacity gains are mostly illusory.

Yet, times change. In itself, a decision to provide a walkway alongside trains in tunnels increases the diameter of the tunnel to be excavated. On the Jubilee Line extension, this puts the diameter up to 4,350mm, for tube stock. Though not relevant for the Jubilee, an operational interface with Railtrack lines would also have an effect. If running over Railtrack is contemplated in part, will overhead electrification (and the space it takes) be preferred throughout? Is the use of mainline rolling stock feasible so that a range of through services can be achieved?

Just as the Thameslink 2000 plans for revitalising the Farringdon-Blackfriars link of Railtrack would never be considered for tube gauge, there may be other opportunities where at least surface gauge should be contemplated. Old certainties may need to be re-examined in future developments.

Below: **The District Line junction at Turnham Green became grade separated in 1912. Chiswick Park station is at the higher level to the left of the picture. A D stock train takes the Richmond branch on 21 March 1990; it will soon reach the breaks in the conductor rails which mark the end of London Underground and the beginning of Railtrack ownership.**

2
TODAY'S ORGANISATION

The London Regional Transport Act 1984 created the body of that name, which nowadays prefers to be known as London Transport. From 29 June 1984, London Regional Transport ceased to be responsible to the Greater London Council and reported instead to the Secretary of State for Transport. LRT is a statutory corporation, whose duties are set out in s2 of that Act:

'It shall be the general duty of London Regional Transport, in accordance with principles from time to time approved by the Secretary of State...to provide or secure the provision of public transport services for Greater London (s2(1)).'

In carrying out that duty, London Regional Transport shall have due regard to: 'the transport needs for the time being of Greater London; and efficiency, economy and safety of operation (s2(2)).'

Further requirements (as amended by the Railways Act 1993) relate to the duties of LRT and the Franchising Director for National Railways services to co-operate with each other in co-ordinating the passenger transport services in London (s2(3A)). It is a duty of LRT to control the general level and structure of fares and service frequencies (s8). The Franchising Director is under a similar duty to consult with LRT on the rail services under his control (s31A).

LRT's financial duty is to ensure that its total income, including grants, is sufficient to meet all its expenses, taking one year with another (s15). The Act empowers the Secretary of State to make grants for capital investment and to help cover operation costs.

The revenue budget specifies targets for the total level of service provision, income and costs. Revenue support grant has not been required since 1993/4. In 1997/8, gross margins from the present businesses are expected to contribute a net total of £184 million.

The capital budget covers investment in new or extended railway lines, replacement rolling stock and other equipment, and in infrastructure. The grant paid to LT comes from Central Government. The LT Annual Business Plan for 1997/8 shows that the Government grant is £701 million in the 1997/8 financial year. Net of £58 million carried forward from 1996/7, the grant is to be spent as follows:

■ £400 million towards the £763 million core business capital investment programme;
■ £295 million ring-fenced expenditure on the Jubilee Line Extension;

Below: **Organisation chart of LRT as at March 1997.**

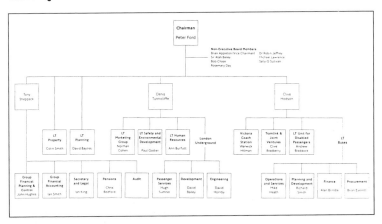

■ £50 million to facilitate construction of Croydon Tramlink;
■ £2 million initial work at King's Cross for Channel Tunnel Rail Link connection;
■ £12 million for Dial-a-Ride bus services.

The £763 million core business capital programme is made up as follows:

■£337 million London Underground network investment, including track, signalling, bridges, tunnelling, power supply;
■ £37 million for London Transport Buses;
■ £13 million for other LT Group investment;
■ £376 million for Jubilee Line Extension core work.

The prospect of a continued reduction in Government grants, as outlined by the then Chancellor in November 1996, of which this reflects the first year, will reduce network investment by some £700 million in the period to 1999/2000.

This excludes any investment under the Private Finance Initiative (PFI). In addition to the above, the private sector will be investing an estimated £130 million in 1997/8 on new Northern Line trains, while a deal to modernise the Underground's power supply system could represent a further £30 million in that year.

Investments by other parties still have to be paid for, and the result is to transfer the expenditure on capital goods to the revenue budget.

London Transport's present key strategies are:

■ to increase public transport's market share through stimulating new travel, attracting traffic from the private car and retaining existing customers;
■ to improve the satisfaction of existing and new customers;
■ to continue to give the highest priority to safety and security;
■ to mitigate the impact of investment reductions and work towards service quality and financial targets agreed with Government;
■ to ensure a successful opening of the Jubilee Line Extension;
■ to increase the contribution made to improving London's environment; and
■ to plan towards achieving Modern Transport for London.

Presently, London Regional Transport has two subsidiary companies. London Underground Ltd was set up in 1985 as a wholly-owned subsidiary to operate the Underground railway network. The other subsidiary is Victoria Coach Station Ltd. An organisation diagram is included on page 11.

London Underground is a major business, with 2.5 million passengers a day, some 470 trains, 245 stations, 16,010 staff and very extensive engineering assets. The core activity is the provision of passenger services which operate for 19hr per day (05.30-00.30), managed through eight General Managers. Each is responsible for one, two or three of the 12 Underground lines.

Of LUL's staff (excluding contractors), the major divisions in 1996/7 were:

■ Passenger services	11,476	72%
■ Engineering	3,094	19%
■ Jubilee Line Extension	680	4%
■ Police	478	3%
■ Other	282	2%

The company is discussed in subsequent sections.

Travel Information

A London Transport activity which impacts substantially upon the Underground is the Travel Information Service. This is a telephone enquiry bureau, which also arranges for teletext broadcasts and information for local radio stations. There are also 13 travel information centres.

Over 3.7 million telephone enquiries are received each year, and the number is growing fast. Research

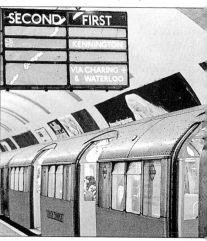

indicates that over two-thirds of those who make a telephone call actually make the journey concerned and that 13% would not have otherwise made the journey. The revenue benefits cover the cost of providing the information by a factor of four.

Analysis of the subject of calls shows that 32% concern journey planning, which have been the most time consuming to deal with. Others are timetables (33%), fares (19%) and other (16%). This last covers anything from lost property to bicycles and the mobility impaired.

The computerised ROUTES (Rail Omnibus Underground Travel Enquiry System) allows the telephone enquiry bureau and also travel information centres to offer a detailed itinerary between any two addresses in Greater London. Those involving multi-modal journeys with up to three interchanges take 12sec to be prepared; more interchanges take a little longer. Customers may specify features such as quickest route, minimum number of interchanges, via or avoiding a particular point, or limiting the number of travel zones. Even, dare one say it, avoiding use of the Underground. There is also an overlay of real time information about service disruption and engineering works.

Disabled

The Unit for Disabled Passengers acts as a focal point within London Transport for co-ordinating initiatives to make transport more accessible to people with disabilities. This includes all those with disabilities, not merely those confined to wheelchairs. The fitting of induction loops at ticket offices has helped the hard of hearing, and textured surfaces those with visual impairments. There are also people with what might be termed self-inflicted disabilities, such as large quantities of luggage, or those with pushchairs, shopping and small children.

The Jubilee Line Extension has been designed to be fully accessible for wheelchairs. More Underground rolling stock is now fitted with audible door closing warnings and verbal announcements of the next station and the train's destination. Lifts, too. At Regent's Park, a disembodied voice suggests turning left from the station exit to reach Harley Street, or right for London Zoo. In the downward direction, one is instructed to turn right for Piccadilly Circus and left for Baker Street.

It is also planned to develop a network of stations at which step-free access (including by lift) will be provided

Above: A wheelchair is about to be followed onto a Docklands Light Railway train at Shadwell by a pushchair; both reached the platform by lift. Note the lack of a gap between platform and train — an example of the possibilities of a more user-friendly design for the Underground's new stations.

Left: A Northern Line train indicator, traditional style, at Camden Town with a 1959 stock train. This system had many merits, but it did not give any indication as to how long the passenger might need to wait. It was hardly a hi-tech method, but it did work.

Above: London Underground deems it necessary to add a warning to the platform edge at Chalfont & Latimer for the Chesham bay, though the gap is minimal for the Underground.

Above: Regent's Park station has gained an apostrophe since the tiling was carried out.

to make the Underground more user friendly and expand its market. All other new lines and extensions will be fully accessible and, whenever practicable, major refurbishment of existing stations will incorporate step-free access from the street to the platforms.

Regulations under the Disability Discrimination Act 1995 are being drawn up for new rail vehicles (and also buses). The aim is to make it possible for disabled persons to get on or off rail vehicles in safety and without unreasonable difficulty, and to be carried on them in safety and reasonable comfort. Those using wheelchairs are included in the above, with the proviso that they should be able to remain in their wheelchairs while travelling. There may also be regulations including equipment to be carried, the space to be provided for wheelchairs, and assistance to be given (s46).

New vehicles entering service from a date to be determined will require accessibility as above. However, in the case of trains, the problem of infrastructure at stations needs equally to be addressed. This is covered under access to premises and the duties of service providers (s21).

It is much easier to justify expenditure when it can be seen to benefit a large part of the business's market. Thus, level boarding of trains speeds joining and alighting times at stations; ultimately, journey time is reduced and higher service frequencies can be offered to the greater number of people who are attracted to use the enhanced service. Everybody wins, but it doesn't help to gain access to the platform in the first place. Although the payback period may be calculated, it will be long term; the capital expenditure is required up front. Public monies are necessary, as there will always be other investments offering more attractive returns.

Property

London Transport Property identifies opportunities for generating income from property and property-related activities. Among its activities, LT Property provides policy guidance on major projects such as the Jubilee Line Extension and the Northern Line modernisation.

At the planning stage, LT Property advises on the property implications of a project, produces land cost estimates, advises on town planning and rating issues and exploits any development opportunities created. It subsequently acquires any land needed by compulsory purchase or agreement, and undertakes the property work involved.

In addition to the sale of surplus operational property, LT Property aims to identify and exploit development opportunities on, over and beside operational land and buildings. Development produces capital and revenue income, but can also offer passenger benefits. The 41,800sq m Broadway Centre development at Hammersmith is fully let and provides major new transport interchange facilities with a new bus station and Underground station ticket hall.

However, commercial uses have to be of fairly high value and high density in central areas, to pay for the cost of rafting over Underground infrastructure. Several storeys are essential; for one or two storeys it is far cheaper to build elsewhere.

A major deal has been completed for the development of surplus land above the Central Line depot at White City for a regional shopping centre of 65,000sq m. This development will provide LT with capital and revenue income, a new bus station and improvements to the railway depot.

LT Property is responsible also for income from shop rentals at stations as well as vending machines, telephones, etc.

LT Museum

The Covent Garden museum in the former Flower Market is a non-profit-making independent organisation, owned and operated by London Transport.

The focus of the museum is the major developments in travel in London and in London's transport history. There are extensive displays of Underground, tram, bus and trolleybus hardware from earlier years.

There are also historical reference facilities.

Not all items of historical interest are to be found in the LT Museum; around 50 of London Underground's stations and other structures are Grade II listed by English Heritage.

Above: Hammersmith District and Piccadilly Line station has been totally rebuilt in recent years. This is the view looking east from the westbound Piccadilly platform, with a 1973 stock train disappearing into the distance.

Right top: The London Transport Museum contains Metropolitan Railway Beyer Peacock 4-4-0T 'A' class locomotive No 23, though it was residing in the former British Transport Museum at Clapham when photographed. By 1886, 120 had been built, of which 66 were for the Metropolitan and 54 for the Metropolitan District.

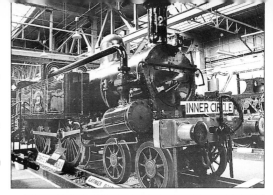

Right: The Grade II listed Arnos Grove station, a Charles Holden design, opened in 1932.

Above: The first occasion on which a train has been painted in an advertising livery occurred on 19 June 1995. The train of 1973 Piccadilly Line stock in United Airlines colours is seen arriving at Acton Town from Heathrow Terminals 1, 2, 3.

Right: At Woodside Park, the former goods yard has been turned into a car park, seen on the right of the approaching Northern Line train of 1959 stock bound for Kennington via Charing Cross.

3
THE UNDERGROUND BUSINESS

Use of the Underground, and indeed all public transport in London, is dependent upon many factors. Certainly, the state of the national economy in general, and that of London in particular, are key indicators. As many as 40% of journeys in London each day are directly related to work, and many others are trips by customers to obtain goods and services.

Around one million people work in central London. Roughly one-third of that workforce lives in inner London, a third in outer London, and the rest elsewhere in the southeast region. This places a large load on the public transport services, the journeys on which are strongly radial in nature.

But off-peak travel has increased, with more leisure, shopping and education trips being made. Tourism has also grown, while more flexible working hours have spread what might otherwise have been peak loads. The off-peak market responds strongly to service improvements, as it is particularly responsive to the cost, comfort and convenience of travel. There may also be more choice of how to make the journey.

The table below shows how the total passenger km travelled on the Underground has changed in recent years, and what has happened to service provision over the same period:

London Underground: passenger demand and service production

Year	Pass km (millions)	as index 1972=100	Train km (millions)	as index 1972=100
1972	5,345	100	48	100
1977	4,344	81	48	100
1982	3,653	68	47	98
1987/88	6,257	117	51	106
1992/93	5,758	108	53	110
1997/98	6,440	120	65	135

Projections for 1997/8 are from the Annual Business Plan.

Above: D stock trains at Tower Hill. The arriving train on the right is for Upminster; the train in the centre bay platform is about to depart for Richmond.

Below right: Crowds await the arriving westbound Central Line 1962 stock train at 08.15 at Stratford in May 1991. Many will have transferred from a train originating at Southend Central or Shenfield on the other side of the island platform.

The 1970s saw a steady decline in Underground usage, which was accompanied by, if not necessarily caused by, higher fares in real terms. It was not, however, matched by proportionate service adjustments.

Fares Fair

For London Transport, the early 1980s were dominated by the 'Fares Fair' débâcle. These were the later years under the control of the Greater London Council. The series of events was as follows:

On 4 October 1981, fares were lowered by 32%, in fulfilment of an electoral pledge by the incoming Greater London Council earlier that year. As a result, passenger volumes rose by 10%, but fares revenue went down by 25%. The contribution by ratepayers rose by £125 million per annum.

The Greater London Council's policy of reduced fares was challenged in the Divisional Court by the London Borough of Bromley, and the initial judgement was in favour of the GLC.

However, in the Court of Appeal and then in the House of Lords, five Law Lords ruled on 17 December 1981 that the reduced fares were unlawful, from their interpretation of the Transport (London) Act 1969, particularly having regard to the fiduciary duty of the Greater London Council towards its ratepayers.

The GLC agreed, early in 1982, that fundamental changes in policy had to be accepted, in particular:
■ that passenger fares should be increased by the maximum practicable extent at the earliest practical date;
■ that levels of service should be reduced to the maximum extent which would reduce costs in order to break even 'so far as practicable'; and
■ that every possible economy had to be pursued in 1982 and beyond.

On 21 March 1982, fares were nominally doubled, but in fact were raised by 96%. Passenger volumes dropped by 18%, revenue rose by 65%, and ratepayers' contributions fell by £206 million in a full year.

Traffic fell away, and passenger journeys on the Underground in 1982 dropped below 500 million, a record low point in recent years. For London Transport as

18

a whole, this was the largest instant decrease in traffic ever.

However, as the then Chairman, Sir Peter Masefield, said in LT's Annual Report for 1981, this left no clear answers to the following questions:

■ What fares are acceptable, taking account of the needs of the community?
■ What level of service should be provided?
■ What amount of subsidy can be made available for both capital and revenue purposes, and from whom?

The 'Fares Fair' policy had been applied equally to buses and the Underground. Indeed, the cover of the Annual Report carried aerial pictures of the Houses of Parliament (and a D stock train with Westminster on the blind) and County Hall (with a Routemaster bus showing that as its destination). However, it is fair to point out that LB Bromley has buses but no Underground stations, and also that Bromley rail users received no equivalent fares benefits on their journeys by the then British Rail. In this, of course, they were not alone. Of the 32 London Boroughs, six have no Underground stations at all, and a pair have two only. All of these are south of the Thames, if one includes Richmond which is the only borough to span the river.

The next move with fares was a December 1982 decision by the Greater London Council to implement a scheme of fares simplification and integration, which would reduce fares by about 25% on 22 May 1983. A High Court declaration was first obtained to test the legality of this decision. The simplification referred to was Travelcard, giving unrestricted travel on buses and on the Underground within the fare zones paid for. (British Rail services were not fully incorporated until 1989.) It was, though, the end of the Greater London Council's involvement, since on 29 June 1984, London Transport was transferred to the control of the Secretary of State for Transport, as already related.

Today's Fares System

Ordinary tickets are purchased at an Underground station before starting a journey. There are different rates for adults and for children aged five and under 16. Children under five travel free.

Single fares are available between any two points and do not vary by time of day. Same day return tickets are twice the single fare.

London is divided into six ticket zones, which are concentric. Central Zone 1 covers the Circle Line plus Euston, Aldgate East, Vauxhall and Earl's Court, while Zone 6 includes Heathrow, West Ruislip, Epping and Upminster.

A booklet of Carnet tickets comprises 10 single Underground tickets for Zone 1, which have a 12-month validity. These must be purchased from a ticket office.

It is often forgotten, but tickets are sold subject to conditions of travel. These are set out in a booklet issued free and available from Underground ticket offices.

Travelcard

Travelcard tickets, which cover travel on the Underground, Docklands Light Railway, buses and National Railways for nearly all journeys within Greater London, are available for different groups of (adjacent) fare zones and for different time periods.

One Day Travelcards are available for use only after 09.30 on Mondays to Fridays, or at any time on Saturdays, Sundays and Bank Holidays. A relatively new product, the LT Card, has no time restrictions, but is not available on National Railways (except where they run in parallel with LUL).

A Weekend Travelcard takes the conditions of a One Day Travelcard, but is valid for two consecutive weekend days. The Family Travelcard is another One Day variant for up to two adults with up to four children.

The Period Travelcard, which has no time restrictions, is available for any period of seven days or any period between one month and one year, including odd days.

Period Travelcard users, both adult and child, must hold a photocard (the number of which is entered on the Travelcard) to validate their ticket. Child photocards are also required for those aged 14 and 15 when purchasing other ticket types.

Other ticketing products of relevance to the Underground are:

■ Point to point season tickets which cross zonal boundaries where the Travelcard fare is inappropriate.
■ Zone extension tickets, issued before commencing a journey, where a Travelcard or LT Card holder wishes to make a journey which goes beyond the boundary of their card.
■ Through tickets via London, London tickets with Travelcard or other London Underground additions issued at National Railways stations outside Greater London.
■ Underground journeys which extend beyond Moor Park into Hertfordshire or Buckinghamshire outside Zone 6, where different fares apply.

There are further products which are not available generally. These include tickets for Visitors; Concessionary Travel Permits for the Elderly, Blind and Disabled; tickets for Local Education Authorities; for staff use; for contractors and for other site visitors.

Travelcard was an immediate and outstanding success, to the extent that it engendered a traffic growth which was around double that anticipated. In social cost-benefit terms, for every £1 revenue lost through fares reduction, it was estimated that the benefits in terms of lower fares, extra travel and reduced road congestion were worth £2.30.

Nearly 15 years after its introduction, Travelcard has strengthened its hold: in 1994/5, it was estimated that an average 988,000 Travelcards (One Day and Period types together) were in daily use, and that they accounted for very nearly three-quarters of the journeys made on London Underground.

This later buoyancy has been achieved despite a growth in fare levels in real terms; London Transport's policy has been to raise fares gently, making funds available to improve services. The continued growth of train km in recent years is indeed a major change in service provision.

```
London Underground ⊖ London Underground      ⊖

   15MCH97      CSN 01DAY  RAILCD TRVLCRD STD

   15 MCH 97              »123456«

   & UNDGRD TO=====AMERSHAM/CHESHAM OFF-PEAK

   133560  01  0764    15MCH97 0903    £3:60

 side up • Not for resale    This side up • Not for resale   This
 d subject to conditions – see over  Issued subject to conditions – see over  Issue
```

Left: An Underground One Day all-zone Travelcard. This was issued at White City from a ticket office machine against a Railcard, and includes Amersham and Chesham in its validity.

Present Fares Policy

In December 1991, as recommended by the Monopolies and Mergers Commission, London Transport published a full statement of its fares policy objectives. These were:

'to set fares which are perceived to be fair and reasonable, encouraging mobility and access to London's facilities, and to help relieve London's traffic and environmental problems, while reflecting the cost of providing and operating services. LT believes that fares should be increased modestly in real terms, so that revenue will, over a period of time, match operating costs, including depreciation of assets.'

This general statement of policy has been refined in LT's current marketing plan as follows:

■ Objective 1: to increase the level of fares only where the additional revenue generated can be used to fund service improvements with greater benefits.

■ Objective 2: to achieve a simple fares structure which is easy to understand and communicate, and gives existing and potential customers confidence in using public transport.

■ Objective 3: to increase demand by targeting market segments with niche products that meet specific commercial needs.

The mix of traffic in recent years has changed significantly; passenger journeys are still below the peak of the late 1980s, but passenger km set a new record in 1995/6, signifying a rise in the average journey length.

Underground Usage

Use of the Underground is still dominated by the Monday to Friday peaks, defined as 07.00-10.00 and 16.00-19.00. During the seven day week 49% of all Underground trips take place in these two periods, plus 25% in the inter-peak period and 8% in the evenings. This leaves just 18% of trips taking place at weekends, with Sunday levels only two-thirds those of Saturdays. As to when people travel, most of the weekday growth has been in the evenings.

The journeys people make on the Underground are dominated by work-related trips, either commuting or on employer's business (52%). Social reasons are the next most common reason, with personal business, shopping and visiting friends and relations all around 10%. Overall, education purposes are the least common, though these depend significantly on time and place.

A third of all Underground journeys take place wholly within Zone 1, and nearly half are radial journeys between Zone 1 and another zone. This leaves relatively few journeys which do not involve Zone 1 in one way or

Below: 1972 MkII stock in corporate livery arrives at Willesden Junction Railtrack station on a Bakerloo service to Piccadilly Circus on 28 December 1996. This was during the period when services were suspended southwards due to engineering work on the tunnels under the Thames.

Above: Waterloo has a large transfer to the Bakerloo Line and this view of the northbound platform shows a 1972 MkII stock train arriving in the morning peak.

another. Clearly, the Underground is seen and used as a means of getting around central London and for morning journeys in from the suburbs, both inner and outer, and back again in the evening peak.

The bus is the short distance mode and the Underground is used for the relatively longer distance passenger journeys. Average for the Underground is 8.1km; for bus 3.4km. This reflects the disincentive of a disproportionate access time to the platform for a short journey, and exiting at the other end. A negligible proportion of bus journeys exceed 10km, but nearly a third of Underground passengers travel this distance or more. It is, after all, on the longer journey that the speed of the Underground can be exploited to the full.

Very nearly half of all tickets, as measured by the number of transactions, are sold in the central Zone 1 area, though they account for only a third in terms of value. Zone 2 accounts for a further 24% of transactions, measured both by number and by value. Cash purchases still make more than 75% of total sales, though credit and debit cards are replacing cheques. Passengers are gradually being weaned onto purchasing tickets themselves direct from machines, particularly single fares, but there is still a long way to go.

Three-quarters of London Underground trips are made by London residents, London for that purpose being defined as within the M25. Social classes ABC1 account for as many as three-quarters of Underground users. In age terms, the younger age groups are well represented, especially the 25-34 group. Use of the Underground by the over-60s is relatively slight. These comparisons are made taking into account the composition of London's population as a whole. Finally, in case you wondered, males make just over half of all Underground journeys, but only 41% of those on the buses.

Yet, the Underground must not get carried away by its obvious success in the radial and central London markets in which it, combined with National Railways in some areas, is very strong. If all journeys within London by some means of powered transport are taken into account, the car is dominant, especially for journeys wholly within outer London. In this overall market, modal shares divide as shown opposite.

What, then, should be done to improve the rail system in London, and particularly the Underground? London Transport's 1995 view was:

- Increase train services, as is presently under way.
- Bring the existing worn-out infrastructure up to modern standards, including the station refurbishment programme, which the Chancellor's November 1996 budget statement seemed likely to frustrate.
- Provide new or refurbished trains on all lines. These are discussed later; shortly, only the District Line will be left with unrefurbished stock on most of its services.
- Improve passenger information at stations and platforms.
- Explore joint opportunities with Railtrack.

Market share, by mode, all journeys within Greater London

	%
Bus	20
Underground	9
National Railways	4
Car, as driver or passenger	63
Taxi, minicab, m/cycle, cycle	4
Total	**100**

Below: Crowds join a westbound C stock Circle Line outer rail train at the old Mansion House station, using the four pairs of sliding doors per car side in the way in which they were intended.

THE UNDERGROUND, LINE BY LINE

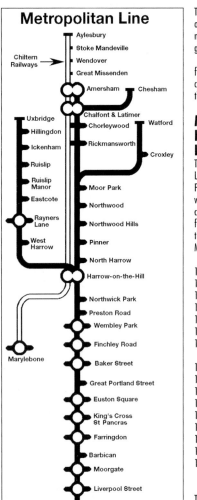

Metropolitan Line

Aylesbury
Stoke Mandeville
Chiltern Railways →
Wendover
Great Missenden
Amersham — Chesham
Chalfont & Latimer
Uxbridge
Chorleywood — Watford
Hillingdon
Rickmansworth
Ickenham
Croxley
Ruislip
Ruislip Manor
Moor Park
Eastcote
Northwood
Rayners Lane
Northwood Hills
West Harrow
Pinner
North Harrow
Harrow-on-the-Hill
Northwick Park
Preston Road
Wembley Park
Finchley Road
Marylebone
Baker Street
Great Portland Street
Euston Square
King's Cross St Pancras
Farringdon
Barbican
Moorgate
Liverpool Street
Aldgate

The Underground is divided into a series of 12 lines, each of which is identified by its own name and colour. In management terms however, there are only eight groups.

Each line is discussed in turn, with the surface lines first. All references are to the lines as they exist today; closed sections and closed stations have been omitted in the descriptions.

Metropolitan Line, including the Hammersmith & City and Circle Lines

The Metropolitan Railway pioneered the Underground in London with its initial 1863 line between Paddington and Farringdon. Success soon had the concept extended, both within and then outside the presently built-up area. The construction resulted in a network which today extends for 89.12km and serves 54 stations. (Only the parts of the Circle Line which are coterminous with other Metropolitan Line services are included here.)

The railway opened as follows:

1863 Paddington-Farringdon
1864 Paddington-Hammersmith
1865 Farringdon-Moorgate
1868 Baker Street-Swiss Cottage (Metropolitan)
1875 Moorgate-Liverpool Street
1876 Liverpool Street-Aldgate
1879 Swiss Cottage (Metropolitan)-Willesden Green (Metropolitan)
1880 Willesden Green-Harrow-on-the-Hill
1884 Liverpool Street-Whitechapel
1885 Harrow-on-the-Hill-Pinner
1887 Pinner-Rickmansworth
1889 Rickmansworth-Chesham
1892 Chalfont & Latimer-Amersham (-Aylesbury)
1904 Harrow-on-the-Hill-Uxbridge
1925 Moor Park-Watford
1936 Whitechapel-Barking (first served by Metropolitan)

The description covers, initially, a journey from Aldgate to Amersham.

Above: The centre platforms here at Baker Street are used principally by through trains to Aldgate. A train of A stock is arriving.

Below: Above Baker Street station is Chiltern Court, flats built in lieu of what was intended by the Metropolitan Railway to be a hotel. They date only from 1929.

From Aldgate, a subterranean station with two island platforms at which the centre tracks are termini, a westbound or inner rail train negotiates the junction and proceeds towards Liverpool Street and Moorgate. At the latter, there are two additional terminal platforms. An underground section extends from west of Liverpool Street through to Barbican. Daylight ensues for a period, then from the approaches to King's Cross St Pancras, the line is almost continuously underground until Finchley Road, apart from some of Baker Street station itself and a short section across the Grand Union Canal.

This part of Baker Street is a four-platformed station, the centre tracks being used normally for services to and from the City, the other two for terminating trains.

From Finchley Road, the Metropolitan trains take the outer tracks and run nonstop to Wembley Park or, in some cases, to Harrow-on-the-Hill. A 12min journey time by the Jubilee to Wembley Park takes 6min by the Metropolitan, which encourages interchange between the lines.

From Wembley Park there are four Metropolitan Line tracks to Harrow, with the Uxbridge and Watford trains taking the local lines and calling at Preston Road and Northwick Park.

Harrow-on-the-Hill has six platforms, it being also the first station at which the Chiltern Line trains, up to now confined to their own tracks, stop. With the loss of the Uxbridge services via a diveunder, the four tracks still continue. Generally, the main line is allocated to Amersham and Chiltern Line

Left: **Line depots undertake train overhaul themselves. This is Ruislip on 15 March 1997, with a 1962 stock DM undergoing a body lift and a 1992 stock car alongside.**

Aylesbury trains, and the local line with the intermediate stations through Pinner and Northwood to Watford services.

After Watford South Junction, the shared two tracks which remain continue to Rickmansworth, which has sidings and turnback facilities; Chalfont & Latimer, junction for Chesham; and Amersham. This happens to double as the highest station on the Underground, 147m above sea level. It was a long slog into the Chilterns for steam-hauled trains, which came to an end with line electrification in 1961.

Of the mainline branches, that from Harrow to Uxbridge meets the Piccadilly Line at Rayners Lane where a turnback is available for the Piccadilly. A trailing connection beyond Ruislip station provides access to Ruislip depot. Uxbridge terminus has three platforms; the rolling stock sidings on the north side of the line are broadly on the site of an earlier terminus.

Watford trains via Croxley cross the Grand Union again, but on a massive viaduct this time! There is a single terminus island platform and two sidings, with run-round facilities.

There is also a curve linking Rickmansworth directly towards Watford (Watford North Curve), but this sees minimal passenger train use.

The Chesham branch operates as a shuttle service to and from Chalfont, where it connects into and out of the Amersham line trains, but only incidentally with those of Chiltern Railways. This runs from a bay platform at Chalfont on what is nowadays no more than an extended siding. There are, however, still through trains between Chesham and the City at peaks.

The Hammersmith & City Line starts at the three platform faces of Hammersmith Metropolitan Railway station (or so it says in brick on the station frontage).

Hammersmith depot is on the right, north of the station. Built mostly on viaduct, the line uses Platforms 15 and 16 at Paddington main line. Then into tunnel, it merges with the Circle and District at Praed Street Junction.

Edgware Road has two open-air island platforms, which enable the District trains from Wimbledon to terminate here clear of the Hammersmith & City services. There are also car sidings.

Baker Street Platforms 5 and 6 have been refurbished in a re-creation of the original 1863 style.

The line then continues to Aldgate Junction as already covered, then underground to Aldgate East where the District Line is joined in a trailing junction. With St Mary's Curve leading to the East London Line on the right, the open-air station of Whitechapel is soon reached. A layout similar to Edgware Road allows Hammersmith & City trains to terminate here or continue to Barking.

The line goes underground again to Mile End, where interchange with the Central Line is available, then to the surface at Bromley-by-Bow and stations to Barking. A combination of flyovers and diveunders ensures that Underground trains are kept clear of the LTS services but still provide good interchange with them. A single platform offers terminating facilities, but there are also sidings beyond the station.

The Circle Line shares tracks with other lines, apart from the very short section between Aldgate and Minories Junction, and between High Street Kensington and Gloucester Road. The total route covered is 20.72km and there are 27 stations. The round trip running time is 48min.

The average distance between stations is thus 0.77km and the average speed 26km/h.

The Metropolitan main line carried 110,000 originating passengers in 1995, and half as many again interchanged to the line. The Hammersmith & City carried 100,000, to which those interchanging added 45,000. The Circle Line result was 170,000 passengers and 50,000 interchanging. The combined result was 530,000 passengers using these lines in the course of a year.

Where the difference lies is in the length of journey. Metropolitan main line passengers travel an average 11km, by some margin the greatest of any Underground line, whereas the Hammersmith & City or Circle passenger's average journey is no more than 5km. This illustrates the importance of passenger km as a measure of what is being achieved, as well as passenger journeys. While longer journeys require more vehicles to maintain frequencies and use of infra-structure to achieve them, they also result in higher revenue yields where fares are related to distance travelled.

The busiest section of the line is that between Baker Street and Great Portland Street, where 27,300 travel in the peak three hours and 65,600 all day on an average weekday.

Car feeder traffic is around 50% of customers at Chalfont & Latimer, Chorleywood and Moor Park. All of these stations are beyond the Greater London boundary.

In terms of National Railways' stations, the Metropolitan and H&C lines serve West Ham, Liverpool Street, Moorgate, King's Cross, St Pancras and Paddington. They also come tantalisingly close to Euston. Stations from Harrow northwards have a joint service in a different sense, as also perhaps does Barking.

King's Cross St Pancras and Liverpool Street are both in the top five London Underground stations as measured by traffic levels. Excluding those interchanging, they together account for over 80 million

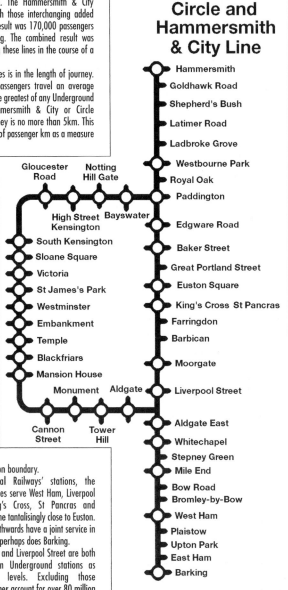

Circle and Hammersmith & City Line

- Hammersmith
- Goldhawk Road
- Shepherd's Bush
- Latimer Road
- Ladbroke Grove
- Westbourne Park
- Royal Oak
- Paddington
- Edgware Road
- Baker Street
- Great Portland Street
- Euston Square
- King's Cross St Pancras
- Farringdon
- Barbican
- Moorgate
- Liverpool Street
- Aldgate East
- Whitechapel
- Stepney Green
- Mile End
- Bow Road
- Bromley-by-Bow
- West Ham
- Plaistow
- Upton Park
- East Ham
- Barking

Gloucester Road · Notting Hill Gate · High Street Kensington · Bayswater · South Kensington · Sloane Square · Victoria · St James's Park · Westminster · Embankment · Temple · Blackfriars · Mansion House · Monument · Aldgate · Cannon Street · Tower Hill

passengers passing through the Underground barriers in the course of a year. This, of course, relates to all Underground lines at these stations.

All services on the Metropolitan main line are provided by eight-car trains of A60/A62 stock. A total of 41 trains is required for the maximum service on Mondays to Fridays, 29 on Saturdays and 21 on Sundays. To this must be added one four-car train every day, for the Chesham shuttle.

Both the Hammersmith & City Line and the Circle Line use six-car trains of C69/C77 stock. Their maximum combined requirement on Mondays to Fridays is 31 trains, reducing to 28 on Saturdays and 25 on Sundays.

The Line management team for all three services is located at Baker Street.

District Line

The District Railway, or rather the Metropolitan District Railway, was only five years behind the Metropolitan, with which company it had a not altogether happy relationship. The hub of the line is Earl's Court. From here the District has four western branches, one to the north, and one very long route to the east. It is also host to Circle Line trains over its central section.

The District Line serves 60 stations and extends over 63.06 route km. The railway opened as follows. The dates refer to the commencement of Underground services on the routes concerned.

1868 Westminster-Edgware Road
1869 Gloucester Road-West Brompton
1870 Westminster-Blackfriars
1871 Blackfriars-Mansion House, Earl's Court-High
    Street Kensington
1874 Earl's Court-Hammersmith
1877 Hammersmith-Richmond
1879 Turnham Green-Ealing Broadway
1880 West Brompton-Putney Bridge
1882 Aldgate-Tower Hill
1884 Mansion House-Whitechapel
1889 Putney Bridge-Wimbledon
1902 Whitechapel-Upminster
1948 Earl's Court-Kensington Olympia

The large Upminster District Line depot is east of the station, which itself has the three-track/three-platform arrangement common for the Underground. Westbound trains parallel Railtrack's London, Tilbury & Southend line, with the District Line being responsible for serving the intermediate stations to Barking.

The next section is described under the Hammersmith & City Line. From Aldgate East, services are in cut-and-

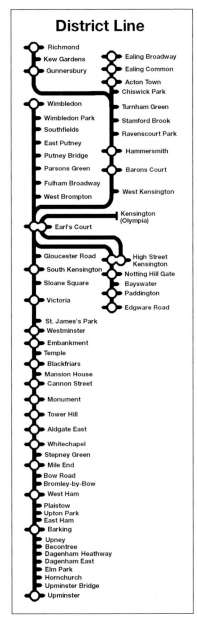

District Line

Richmond
Kew Gardens
Gunnersbury

Ealing Broadway
Ealing Common
Acton Town
Chiswick Park
Wimbledon
Wimbledon Park
Southfields
East Putney
Putney Bridge
Parsons Green
Fulham Broadway
West Brompton

Turnham Green
Stamford Brook
Ravenscourt Park
Hammersmith
Barons Court
West Kensington
Kensington (Olympia)
Earl's Court
Gloucester Road
South Kensington
Sloane Square
Victoria

High Street Kensington
Notting Hill Gate
Bayswater
Paddington
Edgware Road
St. James's Park
Westminster
Embankment
Temple
Blackfriars
Mansion House
Cannon Street
Monument
Tower Hill
Aldgate East
Whitechapel
Stepney Green
Mile End
Bow Road
Bromley-by-Bow
West Ham
Plaistow
Upton Park
East Ham
Barking
Upney
Becontree
Dagenham Heathway
Dagenham East
Elm Park
Hornchurch
Upminster Bridge
Upminster

cover, which has mostly been covered over again. Side platforms, as elsewhere on the surface lines, are usually provided. At Minories Junction, the Circle Line trains join the District tracks. At both Tower Hill and Mansion House, a centrally-located turnback siding with a platform face enables eastbound trains to be reversed.

Beyond South Kensington station, which itself is in daylight, a second westbound track is provided for the Circle Line; this avoids delaying westbound District trains if the Circle train cannot obtain a path across Gloucester Road Junction. The Circle services now turn north to High Street Kensington.

Continuing to Earl's Court, daylight becomes more common. The large two-island station with overall roof provides for up to four simultaneous and non-conflicting movements. This is achieved by two pairs of double tracks approaching from High Street Kensington and from Tower Hill in the east, and from Wimbledon and from Hammersmith in the west, together with two grade-separated junctions.

Taking first the Wimbledon line, a short section under Earl's Court Exhibition Centre emerges into daylight at West Brompton. Fulham Broadway has, again, an overall roof. Emerging from the short tunnel section and climbing onto a viaduct, the train reaches Parsons Green

with a number of rolling stock sidings. At Putney Bridge the centre turnback siding and platform can accommodate a C stock length train only.

After crossing Fulham Bridge over the Thames, the line beyond East Putney may see South West Trains empty rolling stock workings joining the route on their return to Wimbledon Park sidings. East Putney Tunnel (284m) gives way to a suburban run to the Wimbledon terminus. The line is now owned by London Underground, apart from the terminus itself which remains with Railtrack. Connections to the South Western main line remain.

The alternative westwards route from Earl's Court gives access to Kensington Olympia via West Kensington East Junction. This becomes a single track to the terminus, but not before providing a connection to Lillie Bridge Permanent Way Depot. This large facility also has a connection directly onto the District main line. Beyond West Kensington, the Piccadilly rises to the surface between the District tracks and at Barons Court a cross-platform connection between the two lines can be made. The same is true of Hammersmith, more commonly used for this purpose.

The District Line trains then call at all stations and for Richmond turn to the south at Turnham Green. The eastbound junction is grade separated. Railtrack is joined

Below: **The District and Piccadilly lines run parallel for a long stretch to Barons Court, where the Piccadilly goes underground before resurfacing in north London. A train of D stock for Upminster has a 1973 stock train in pursuit as it approaches the station.**

approaching Gunnersbury, and the tracks are shared with North London Railways thence over the Thames to Kew Gardens and Richmond.

Avoiding taking the Richmond branch at Turnham Green, District Line trains reach Acton Town and their large Ealing Common depot is seen on the right. Grade separation allows trains for Ealing Broadway to climb over the westbound Piccadilly Heathrow branch, but the Piccadilly Uxbridge trains take the same route.

The District Line trains take the left-hand option at Hanger Lane Junction, from which they have sole use of the 1km of line into Ealing Broadway. Three platforms are reserved here for their use and there is a physical connection to the Central Line.

Finally, Edgware Road-Wimbledon services leave Earl's Court for High Street Kensington, pass through the middle of Triangle Sidings which are now roofed over, and negotiate an at-grade junction to enter the through platforms on the outer rail. There are also two terminating platforms, useful as a bolt hole for westbound District Line D stock if there are problems on the main line via Tower Hill. They also see some regular scheduled use, traditionally for the shuttle service to Kensington Olympia.

Only C stock is allowed to proceed beyond Kensington High Street, principally due to the short platforms at the ensuing stations. These are cut-and-cover lines, but both Notting Hill Gate and Paddington (Praed Street) are noteworthy for their overall roofs. The District trains terminate at Edgware Road.

This section is shared with the Circle Line, which uses C stock for the same reasons.

The District Line carried 420,000 originating passengers in 1995, at 16.7% of the Underground total which was more than any other line. Another 155,000 interchanged with the District line, making 575,000 annual users.

The busiest section in the peak three hours is from Victoria to St James's Park with 40,200 passengers, although the all day busiest section is in the other direction from Victoria to Sloane Square. In all, 110,500 passengers make this daily journey.

Embankment is among the top 10 busiest LUL stations, with a total annual usage of 39.5 million. However, over half of these are passengers interchanging between lines.

In terms of stations at which trains of National Railways call, the District serves directly Upminster, Barking, West Ham, Tower Hill (for Fenchurch Street), Cannon Street, Blackfriars, Embankment (for Charing Cross), Victoria, Wimbledon, Gunnersbury/Richmond, Ealing Broadway and Paddington.

All services on the District Line apart from the Edgware Road-Wimbledon service are provided by six-car trains of D stock. A total of 66 trains is required for the maximum service on Mondays to Fridays, 51 on Saturdays and 48 on Sundays.

The Edgware Road-Wimbledon service uses six-car trains of C69/C77 stock. The maximum requirement on Mondays to Fridays is 10 trains, reducing to seven on both Saturdays and Sundays.

The Line management team is located near St James's Park station.

East London Line

The East London Line has an exceptional history, being based on the development of the pioneering bored tunnel between Wapping and Rotherhithe, which was completed after many vicissitudes in 1843. Although

Below: New advertising displays are always appearing; this one perhaps is designed to acquaint overseas visitors with English etiquette?

intended for horse-drawn vehicles, the access ramps were never constructed, and its initial use was for pedestrians only.

In 1869, Sir Marc Brunel's twin tunnels were adapted for railway use and progressively extended as the East London Railway. Various companies provided services. These included both the Metropolitan and District Railways from 1884, but these were withdrawn in 1906 and 1905 respectively. The line as it exists today was electrified in 1913, from which time the passenger services were operated by the Metropolitan. There are eight stations and the line covers 7.22km.

The northern terminus, Shoreditch, is located on a single-track stub, and the line's former connection to the Great Eastern Railway and Liverpool Street is clearly visible. Double track is resumed almost immediately on leaving the station. As far as Shadwell, open-air sections are interspersed with tunnels.

During periods when Shoreditch is not served, trains terminate in the northbound platform at Whitechapel. A scissors crossover south of the platforms provides the necessary flexibility. This is succeeded by the trailing Whitechapel Junction, which gives access to St Mary's Curve and the District Line. This is presently the only physical link to the rest of the railway system, and is used for stock movements.

All stations have side platforms. The distance under the Thames from Wapping to Rotherhithe is 0.52km; the lights of a train at the other station can be seen from the platform, reflected on the rails, but the line's vertical curvature prevents the observer from seeing the train itself.

A new station is being constructed at Canada Water, with interchange provided to the Jubilee Line Extension which passes underneath.

Emerging from tunnel, the line enters Surrey Quays station. At Canal Junction, the route to New Cross leaves the earlier line to New Cross Gate. Both lines become single for their last sections into the Railtrack-owned termini.

New Cross rolling stock depot, to which there is no road access, is situated on the New Cross branch.

Service provision has to be managed around the limitations of the single track termini. With a 12min running time between Shoreditch and either southern terminus, a 10tph service over the section to Surrey Quays and 5tph to each of the branches can be maintained comfortably with five trains. Even so, the stand time at Shoreditch is 2min only.

How does London Underground see the East London Line? The following is taken from a 1995 LUL fact sheet: 'For many years, the East London Line had a somewhat ambiguous status as a separate but not altogether autonomous part of the Metropolitan Line. In many ways, it was the poor relation of the Underground,

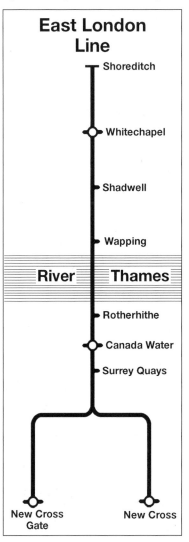

Above: **Wapping has remarkably narrow platforms. An A stock train disappears into the Thames tunnel.**

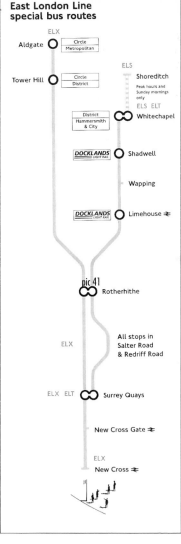

East London Line special bus routes

tucked away in a declining and unglamorous part of London. The line experienced enormous growth during the 1980s, due largely to regeneration and economic growth in Docklands. The line now requires special attention in terms of resources.'

In practice, the East London Line has not operated since March 1995, when it was closed for engineering work, mainly in connection with the Thames Tunnel, but also for the construction of Canada Water station. Replacement bus services have been provided.

Prior to closure, there were 20,000 passenger journeys per day on the line, with another 5,000 interchanging to it.

All Underground services in recent times have been provided by four-car sets of A stock. A total of five trains is required for the maximum service on weekdays, reducing to four or three on Sundays, according to the service being operated.

The East London is managed by the Jubilee Line team.

Bakerloo Line

The Bakerloo is one of the Yerkes tubes, built by the American financier Charles Tyson Yerkes. It is 23.55km long and serves 25 stations between Elephant & Castle and Harrow & Wealdstone. The present line was opened in sections as follows:

1906 Elephant & Castle-Baker Street
1907 Baker Street-Edgware Road
1913 Edgware Road-Paddington
1915 Paddington-Willesden Junction
1917 Willesden Junction-Harrow & Wealdstone

Moving from south to north, the line starts in two stabling sidings south of Elephant & Castle platforms, which could form the beginning of a line extension should that ever be built. Trains start from the underground twin island platform at Elephant & Castle; although not an ideal arrangement, a 3.5min turnround

Bakerloo Line

- Harrow & Wealdstone
- Kenton
- South Kenton
- North Wembley
- Wembley Central
- Stonebridge Park
- Harlesden
- Willesden Junction
- Kensal Green
- Queen's Park
- Kilburn Park
- Maida Vale
- Warwick Avenue
- Paddington
- Edgware Road
- Marylebone
- Baker Street
- Regent's Park
- Oxford Circus
- Piccadilly Circus
- Charing Cross
- Embankment
- Waterloo
- Lambeth North
- Elephant & Castle

is regularly achieved here. A scissors crossover controls the station exit.

North of Lambeth North station, a trailing connection to the northbound line gives access to the surface and London Road depot, an early Bakerloo facility. Trains thus leave the depot and proceed to Waterloo where they enter passenger service, while a crossover between the lines allows southbound trains for the depot to terminate in service at Waterloo.

Plain line continues to Piccadilly Circus, at the north end of which what was once a scissors crossover, but is now trailing only, allows southbound trains to terminate in the southbound platform and return north. This facility was used in 1996/7 during the reconstruction of the under-Thames tunnels.

Baker Street, the former Bakerloo junction for its two routes north, retains the connections to and from what is now the Jubilee Line, but these are not used for passenger services.

At Paddington, there is again a trailing crossover.

A ramp leads to the surface and Queen's Park station, which is owned by Railtrack and operated by North London Railways. The Bakerloo occupies the centre lines of the twin islands; NLR trains on the Euston-Watford dc services use the outer faces. The Underground has a south and a north shed here; Bakerloo trains which continue on Railtrack have first to proceed through the outer roads of the north shed itself. Terminating trains normally use the depot centre roads so to do.

Railtrack owns all the infrastructure north of Queen's Park except for the line depot at Stonebridge Park, which belongs to London Underground. This extensive facility is situated north of the station platforms and east of the running lines; terminating trains are unable to reverse in the platforms and thus run via the depot.

Some trains proceed to Harrow & Wealdstone, nowadays the line terminus. The Bakerloo has not run north of here since 1982 and this is now the limit of fourth rail electrification. A central turnback siding is available north of the station.

One shortcoming of the line layout is the inability to terminate, in a northbound direction, anywhere before Queen's Park, other than by reversing in tunnel on the northbound running line. Effectively, this prevents the operation of services over the in-town section only.

In 1995, the Bakerloo Line carried an average weekday traffic of 170,000 passengers originating on the line. This is 6.7% of the Underground total. When those interchanging to the Bakerloo are added, the total rises to 255,000.

Above: There are only spasmodic opportunities to reverse trains on the Underground. One such opportunity is at Piccadilly Circus Bakerloo Line platforms, where the facility was used during the nine-month rebuilding of the under-Thames tunnels in 1996-7. Trains from the north may reverse in the (southbound) platform to the left and proceed north via the crossover. This northbound train is of the long since departed 1938 stock.

The busiest section of the line in the weekday morning peak is that from Baker Street to Regent's Park, with 24,700 passengers in the peak three hours 07.00 to 10.00. On an all day basis through to 22.00, the busy section shifts to Regent's Park to Oxford Circus, with 63,600 passengers. This puts the Bakerloo well down the list of busy lines. Interestingly, overseas visitors make up 12% of the total Bakerloo Line traffic, one of the highest recorded.

At 4km, the average journey lengths made are short. Mainline rail feeder traffic is heavy, with 27% of Bakerloo users originating from National Railways. Paddington, Marylebone and Waterloo are all relatively poorly sited amongst the main line termini, and it shows. Other direct rail feeders come from Elephant & Castle, Charing Cross and, of course, the northern end of the Bakerloo itself.

Piccadilly Circus is the Bakerloo's busiest station and currently the sixth busiest on London Underground as a whole, with 35.2 million passengers a year entering or leaving the station. However, another 6.4 million interchange between lines, giving a total annual usage of 41.6 million in 1995.

Only seven stations are used exclusively by the Bakerloo; of the others, 10 are owned by Railtrack and eight are managed by other Underground lines.

Services are provided exclusively by the seven-car trains of 1972 MkII stock, including a few conversions from the 1972 MkI variety. A total of 31 trains is required for the maximum service on Mondays to Fridays, reducing to 26 on Saturdays and 20 on Sundays with the full line in operation.

The Line management team is located at Baker Street.

Central Line

The Central London Railway was the pioneer of what became the normal tube line. London has always had an east-west axis, and it is difficult to avoid the conclusion that the Central Line has the plum position, straight through the West End and into the middle of the City. At 71.96km, it is the Underground's longest line, serving 49 stations. Its construction history in terms of opening dates is as follows:

Central Line

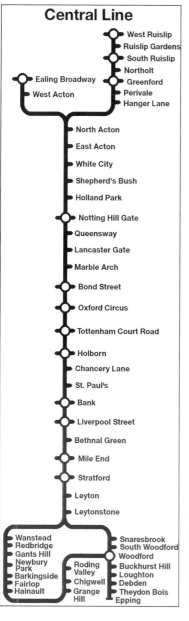

- West Ruislip
- Ruislip Gardens
- South Ruislip
- Northolt
- Greenford
- Perivale
- Hanger Lane
- Ealing Broadway
- West Acton
- North Acton
- East Acton
- White City
- Shepherd's Bush
- Holland Park
- Notting Hill Gate
- Queensway
- Lancaster Gate
- Marble Arch
- Bond Street
- Oxford Circus
- Tottenham Court Road
- Holborn
- Chancery Lane
- St. Paul's
- Bank
- Liverpool Street
- Bethnal Green
- Mile End
- Stratford
- Leyton
- Leytonstone

Wanstead
Redbridge
Gants Hill
Newbury Park
Barkingside
Fairlop
Hainault

Roding Valley
Chigwell
Grange Hill

Snaresbrook
South Woodford
Woodford
Buckhurst Hill
Loughton
Debden
Theydon Bois
Epping

1900 Shepherd's Bush-Bank
1912 Bank-Liverpool Street
1920 Shepherd's Bush-Ealing Broadway
1946 Liverpool Street-Stratford
1947 North Acton-Greenford, Stratford-Woodford/
      Newbury Park
1948 Greenford-West Ruislip, Newbury Park-
      Woodford, Woodford-Loughton
1949 Loughton-Epping

Moving from west to east, the line starts with a connection from Railtrack, used mainly for stock movements to and from Metro-Cammell in Birmingham via the Chiltern Line. A tightly constructed island platform suggests that the line is destined to go further west towards Denham, as indeed was briefly the intention. On the right-hand side between here and Ruislip Gardens is the large car depot.

Stations follow in quick succession. Northolt has a turnback siding for westbound trains; Greenford has a central bay used by Thames Trains' service from Paddington via Ealing Broadway, but there is no physical connection. Hanger Lane nestles (if that is the right word) under that notorious road junction where the North Circular, Hanger Lane and the A40 Western Avenue meet. This is the closest to a tunnel which is met until just beyond White City. The grade-separated North Acton Junction marks the point where the older Ealing Broadway line joins.

The Central Line uses Platforms 5 and 6 at Ealing Broadway; there is a connection to the District Line available. North Acton station now has three platforms, including a loop, for turning trains short. Proceeding east, role reversal takes place with the eastbound and westbound lines changing sides by a flyover 1km short of White City. This 'back to front' station too has a central platform, which leads in the eastbound direction into the depot here. It is used also for service reversals.

The train now dives into tunnel. Apart from an immediate very short respite, open air is not reached until Stratford. The eastbound and westbound lines cross again underground; this reflects the complications imposed by the terminal loop, previously provided here. The stations are mostly islands. Those that are not include Notting Hill Gate, Chancery Lane and St Paul's, which have one line above the other to avoid tunnelling under properties. Turnback sidings for westbound trains may be found in tunnel at Marble Arch and British Museum (west of Holborn at the former station site). All along this stretch of the original Central London, there is ample evidence of the platform lengthening work carried out in the 1930s to accommodate longer trains. The sawtooth construction of track levels used by the CLR to decelerate trains as they arrived and accelerate them away again was not so easily altered.

Beyond Liverpool Street, terminus for over 30 years, there are two sidings between the running lines. Additional short workings between here and Marble Arch or White City have been frequent operating patterns.

At cut-and-cover Mile End, cross-platform interchange to the District Line and Hammersmith & City is available, and there is a shaft of light above the westbound Central Line track. At Stratford, cross-platform is available in both directions with Great Eastern Railway; this is the busiest of all rail-to-Underground interchanges outside central London, with over 9,000 passenger movements per day.

Tunnelling only to pass beneath the main lines, from Leyton onwards the route is over the former GE line which was acquired by LT at the time of what turned out to be the postwar electrification. Many of the stations still bear witness to their history, and the line takes on more the appearance of 'a real railway'. From here northwards, however, the M11 motorway is often uncomfortably close by.

Below: **A 1992 stock train departs from West Ruislip terminus; the Chiltern Lines and a Railtrack signalbox are on the left.**

At three-platformed Leytonstone though, the Hainault branch leaves in tunnel via a burrowing junction; straight on is for Woodford with a few sidings and then the junction for reaching Hainault 'the other way'. Further north are the generously laid out Loughton with sidings for rolling stock, Debden with a reversing facility, and Epping. Shortly before the terminus is reached, the Central Line becomes one of the only two Underground lines to go beyond the M25; the other is the Metropolitan.

The Hainault branch, which we left at Leytonstone, tunnels beneath Eastern Avenue. Cut-and-cover Redbridge is accessed by stairs only, an unusual feature for a pure 'tube' station. Daylight (and the GE) is resumed at Newbury Park. Thence to Hainault the large depot on the west of the line between here and Grange Hill. The 240m Grange Hill Tunnel is the only feature of note on this rural stretch. When the train reaches Woodford Junction, it has reversed itself; to tidy up the direction nomenclature on the loop, the lines are known as inner rail and outer rail, rather than eastbound and westbound.

Railtrack owns Stratford station, but all the remaining infrastructure is owned by London Underground.

The Central Line is provided generously with facilities for short running, which can be used in several combinations. Perhaps the most difficult problem is the mismatch between traffic levels east and west of central London; traffic to the east exceeds considerably the

volumes to the west. In 1995, the Central Line carried an average weekday traffic of 360,000 passengers originating on the line, 14.3% of the total for the Underground. Adding those interchanging to the Central, the combined total is 500,000.

Liverpool Street to Bank is the hardest pressed section of the Central and indeed of the Underground as a whole. In the 3hr morning peak, 40,700 customers are carried on this stretch. For the all day total, the focus moves further west, with 101,300 from Chancery Lane to Holborn for a 16hr traffic day. The Central Line is clearly one of the top performers. A considerable number of longer journeys are made on the Central Line, with 8km being the average distance travelled. It also attracts a large amount of car feeder traffic at the eastern end, with half the passengers at both Epping and Fairlop being car-borne. The only London rail terminus on the Central is Liverpool Street, though passengers for the West End who arrive at Fenchurch Street are likely to walk to Bank. Other stations where interchange with National Railways is available are Stratford, Ealing Broadway, Greenford, South Ruislip and West Ruislip.

Oxford Circus is the really busy station on the Central Line and second busiest on the Underground system, with 53.2 million passengers per year from the entrance/exit counts. Oxford Circus is top for interchange, accounting for another 28.1 million and giving a combined usage of 81.3 million.

All services are provided by the eight-car trains of 1992 stock. A total of 72 trains is required for the maximum service on Mondays to Fridays, reducing to 45 on Saturdays and 38 on Sundays.

The Line management team, who also run the Waterloo & City Line, is located in the vicinity of Lancaster Gate station.

Jubilee Line

The growing suburban traffic in the interwar period on lines to Wembley Park and beyond was becoming an increasing embarrassment to the Metropolitan Railway. With the opening of its Wembley Park-Stanmore branch in 1932, the difficulties of funnelling all traffic into a two-track section south of Finchley Road became ever more apparent.

The solution of the newly formed London Passenger Transport Board was a new extension of the Bakerloo north from Baker Street and completely rebuilding the section beyond Finchley Road, utilising some of the Bakerloo's spare capacity south of Baker Street, and giving Metropolitan passengers a link to the West End.

It was the erosion of the spare element of the Bakerloo's capacity which led to its duplication by the Jubilee Line and the separation which occurred in 1979.

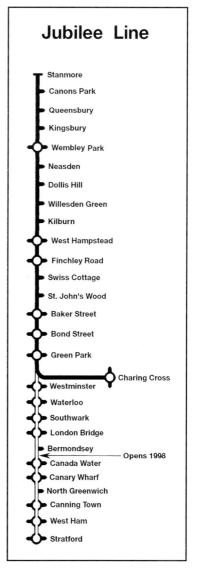

Jubilee Line

- Stanmore
- Canons Park
- Queensbury
- Kingsbury
- Wembley Park
- Neasden
- Dollis Hill
- Willesden Green
- Kilburn
- West Hampstead
- Finchley Road
- Swiss Cottage
- St. John's Wood
- Baker Street
- Bond Street
- Green Park
- Charing Cross
- Westminster
- Waterloo
- Southwark
- London Bridge
- Bermondsey
- Canada Water   ← Opens 1998
- Canary Wharf
- North Greenwich
- Canning Town
- West Ham
- Stratford

The Jubilee, including its new extension, is 40.41km in length and serves 28 stations. Its construction history in terms of opening dates is as follows:

1932 Wembley Park-Stanmore
1939 Baker Street-Wembley Park
1979 Charing Cross-Baker Street
1998 Green Park-Stratford

From Stanmore's island platform and car sidings, the Jubilee Line heads south to Wembley Park. By diving under the southbound Metropolitan tracks it takes up the centre position for Underground services, albeit that Railtrack's Chiltern Line remains on the west side for some time.

Wembley Park has a turnback siding for Jubilee Line northbound services north of the station. On the south side there are junctions to and from the Metropolitan Line tracks and also the vast Neasden depot where trains for both lines are maintained. There are further connections at Neasden.

Jubilee trains serve the island platforms throughout this section; additional turnback sidings for northbound trains are provided both at Willesden Green and West Hampstead. There are further crossovers at the approach to Finchley Road.

Now in tube tunnel, services continue to Baker Street, where same level interchange is available to the Bakerloo for southbound passengers as provided previously. Northbound tracks 'roll over' the southbound to provide an ingenious means of maintaining same-level interchange.

At Green Park a step plate junction has been constructed to allow Extension trains to diverge; the 1979 railway continues to a scissors crossover and the island terminus at Charing Cross. This section is likely to see little use after the Extension is open.

In 1995, the Jubilee Line as it then existed carried an average weekday traffic of 115,000 passengers originating on the line, 4.6% of the Underground's total. Adding those interchanging to the Jubilee, the combined total is 180,000.

The most crowded section was that from St John's Wood to Baker Street, carrying 21,700 passengers in the morning peak period and 47,100 over the day as a whole.

Stanmore is one of the top attractors of car feeder traffic, which accounts for nearly 50% of those boarding there. But the line is most noteworthy for the numbers who walk to its stations, no less than 87% of the total carried and substantially higher than any other Underground line. Presently, Charing Cross and West

Below: The carefully crafted flower display outside St John's Wood station; that roundel gets everywhere!

Hampstead are the only Jubilee Line stations served by National Railways, and interchange volumes are correspondingly small.

Baker Street has a very large volume of interchange between Underground lines at 22 million pa, more in fact than the totals who pass through the ticket barriers. The combined usage of Baker Street for all purposes was 43 million in 1995.

All train services have been provided by the six-car trains of 1983 stock over the last decade or so. A total of 24 trains is required for the maximum service between Stanmore and Charing Cross on Mondays to Fridays, reducing to 18 on Saturdays and 15 on Sundays. The 1996 stock is replacing these trains.

The Line management team, who also run the East London, is located near Bond Street station.

Northern Line

The Northern is a sometimes uncomfortable amalgam of a number of different bits of railway, which was assembled in the 1920s, though the Northern name dates only from 1937. The pioneer City & South London Railway, whatever its other virtues, was in a different dimensions league from what was to follow. The C&SLR was extended over time, northwards to Euston and southwards to Clapham Common.

The other major component was another of the Yerkes tubes, the Charing Cross, Euston & Hampstead Railway, which was both physically and financially a completely separate organisation. The C&SLR and also the Central London Railway were absorbed by the Underground Electric Railways of London (UERL, as the Yerkes tubes had become) in 1913. A major programme of reconstruction, consolidation and extension was completed in 1926.

Finally, part of the former Great Northern Railway was acquired and electrified in 1940/1, while the Great Northern & City, a Metropolitan Railway company but latterly part of the Northern, returned to what was then British Rail in 1975.

Today's Northern Line is 58.12km long and serves 50 stations over its relatively complicated network. The present line was opened in sections, shown here as divided into the three distinct periods:

C&SLR	1890 Stockwell-Borough
	1900 Borough-Moorgate, Stockwell-Clapham Common
	1901 Moorgate-Angel
	1907 Angel-Euston (City line)
CCE&HR	1907 Golders Green/Archway-Charing Cross
	1914 Charing Cross-Embankment

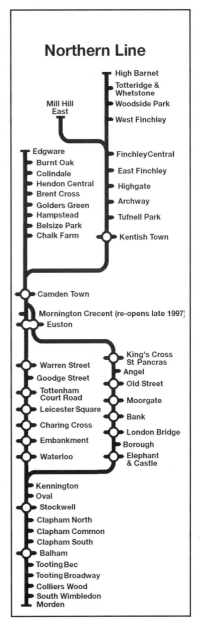

Northern Line

High Barnet
Totteridge & Whetstone
Mill Hill East
Woodside Park
West Finchley
Edgware
Finchley Central
Burnt Oak
East Finchley
Colindale
Hendon Central
Highgate
Brent Cross
Archway
Golders Green
Hampstead
Tufnell Park
Belsize Park
Chalk Farm
Kentish Town
Camden Town
Mornington Crecent (re-opens late 1997)
Euston
King's Cross St Pancras
Warren Street
Angel
Goodge Street
Old Street
Tottenham Court Road
Moorgate
Leicester Square
Bank
Charing Cross
London Bridge
Embankment
Borough
Waterloo
Elephant & Castle
Kennington
Oval
Stockwell
Clapham North
Clapham Common
Clapham South
Balham
Tooting Bec
Tooting Broadway
Colliers Wood
South Wimbledon
Morden

Northern	1923 Golders Green-Hendon Central
	1924 Camden Town-Euston (City line), Hendon Central-Edgware
	1926 Embankment-Kennington, Clapham Common-Morden
	1939 Archway-East Finchley
	1940 East Finchley-High Barnet
	1941 Finchley Central-Mill Hill East

From south to north, the extensive Morden depot is the first to be encountered, then the three-line but five-platform faces of Morden station. Platforms on either side of the train enable arriving and departing passengers to be separated, or at least that is the theory. A similar arrangement exists at Golders Green.

Immediately upon departure, the Northern enters a cut-and-cover section which soon becomes bored tunnel. This lasts all the way to the northern suburbs and via Bank to East Finchley is the longest tunnel on the Underground at 27.8km.

A series of stations with island platforms ensues; at Tooting Broadway there is a turnback siding in tunnel to the south of the station. Normal island platforms are replaced by the narrow variety with no central obstructions at Clapham Common and Clapham North. These are the only ones which still exist in London, though they are standard on the Glasgow Underground.

Stockwell, reconstructed in 1970, offers level interchange between lines in both directions, a feature of the Victoria Line which may also be found on the Northern at Euston City platforms.

Kennington, with side platforms on the City branch, sports two additional platforms for the line from Charing Cross. While trains approaching from Charing Cross may continue to Morden (and vice versa), they may also terminate at Kennington by negotiating the underground loop from Platform 2 (at which they arrive) to Platform 1 (from which they return). Trains via Bank have no such option, though there is a central turnback siding available south of the station.

Continuing all services south of Kennington is not a sustainable option, since this would require up to 20 trains from each of the Charing Cross and City branches to be accommodated on one line. While such traffic levels might be just about achievable in a perfect world, the Northern is not yet that railway. Another complication is the need to remix the trains from each branch at Camden Town depending whether they serve

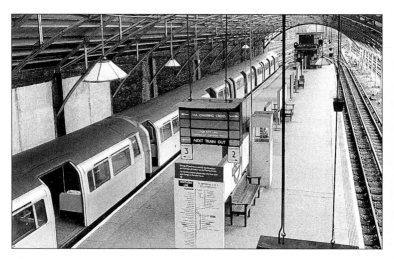

Above: **Many extension plans have been frustrated over the years. Edgware was destined to be a junction station where the line from Finchley Central joined the present Edgware branch of the Northern Line, and the line was to be extended to Elstree. It has never been more than a simple terminus, seen here with a 1972 MkI stock train ready to depart on a service via Charing Cross.**

Edgware or High Barnet/Mill Hill East, given also that running times between Camden Town and Kennington are about 5min longer via Bank.

Neither the Charing Cross branch nor the line via Bank offer much in the way of operating facilities apart from a few trailing crossovers and a facing connection at Euston City line station; for the section Borough to Bank inclusive the northbound rolls over the southbound to provide right-hand running, and then back again, but this is of no practical significance. At Euston City line and at Angel, exceedingly spacious southbound platforms show the effect of removing the constrained island platforms as at the two Clapham stations today.

The Camden Town junctions are comprehensively laid out to avoid conflicting moves, though being underground it is difficult to appreciate their complexity. The Edgware branch has three more deep level stations before reaching the open air at Golders Green. This includes Hampstead, the deepest on the system at 58.2m below ground level.

Golders Green depot is where most maintenance and overhaul work is carried out. Northwards, the Northern Line proceeds on bridging, housing development having already been well advanced before the railway was built. Beyond Hendon Central are the 1km Burroughs Tunnels and at Colindale a turnback siding. Edgware terminus has a three-platform layout, which still shows signs of intended extension which is never likely to take place.

There are car sidings here.

The other Northern Line branch proceeds to Archway, the long-time terminus and still with a turnback siding beyond it. Emerging from tunnel at East Finchley, 52min from leaving Morden, the centre roads of this four-platform station lead only to Highgate depot. Continuing north, Finchley Central has terminating facilities and also a third platform leading to the single-track siding, which is all that remains on the Mill Hill East branch. However, it does include the 18m-high viaduct over the Dollis Brook, the highest point on the Underground system above ground level.

The service continues from Finchley Central to High Barnet, with car sidings and a traditional three-platform layout. Just as the stations at the eastern end of the Central Line are GE in style, the Northern Line is Great Northern for similar reasons.

Operations are a continuing problem, especially if rail traffic continues to grow. Ideas of separating the Northern into two lines would require many people to make interchanges at Camden Town which are presently unnecessary, while the depot facilities would also need expansion. Such a scheme might only be considered realistic if it were associated with an extension of the Charing Cross line to a new destination south of Kennington.

The Northern Line is responsible for carrying an originating traffic of 415,000 passengers on an average

Left: **Highest point above ground level on the Underground is where the Northern Line's Mill Hill East branch crosses the Dollis Brook.**

41

Left: Woodside Park Northern Line station in 1997 is little changed from its appearance before being acquired by the LPTB, whose trains have served it since 1940.

Piccadilly Line

The Piccadilly Line, in its original form the Great Northern, Piccadilly & Brompton, provides a main northeast to southwest link. The total length of line traversed by its trains is 71.27km, in the course of which it serves 51 stations. Its construction history in terms of opening dates is as follows, though both the Uxbridge and Hounslow West extensions from Acton Town were opened much earlier and worked by the District Railway:

weekday, or 16.5% of the Underground total. There are a further 135,000 who interchange to the Northern, making in all 550,000 daily users.

The line's busiest section is that from Clapham North to Stockwell, with 29,600 passengers in the peak three hours, 07.00 to 10.00, and 52,800 on an all day basis. Such levels are not excessive. Bus feeder traffic is significant both at Golders Green and Morden stations; the forecourts of both were laid out extensively for such purposes in the early days. Bus passengers account for 10% of Northern Line customers, which is the system average.

Main line stations directly served are Balham, Waterloo, Charing Cross, Elephant & Castle, London Bridge, Moorgate/Old Street, King's Cross, St Pancras, Euston and Kentish Town. The result is a substantial 14% of Northern Line passengers whose feeder mode to the line is by train.

The average journey length on the Northern is 6km.

Leicester Square is a busy station for the Northern. 27.3 million passengers per year enter or leave the station and another 8.9 million passengers interchange there with the Piccadilly. The total annual usage was 36.2 million in 1995.

For the time being, services are provided by a mixture of the superannuated 1959 and 1962 stock, supplemented by the 1972 MkI stock, all of Metro-Cammell build.

A maximum total of 84 trains is required for service on Mondays to Fridays, which reduces to 59 on Saturdays and 46 on Sundays. New trains of 1995 stock are in the course of delivery and these will provide a complete replacement for the existing trains.

The Line management team is located near Goodge Street.

1906	Finsbury Park-Hammersmith
1932	Finsbury Park-Arnos Grove, Hammersmith-Uxbridge
1933	Arnos Grove-Cockfosters, Acton Town-Hounslow West
1975	Hounslow West-Hatton Cross
1976	Hatton Cross-Heathrow Terminals 1, 2, 3, direct
1988	Hatton Cross-Heathrow Terminals 1, 2, 3 via Terminal 4

Below: The Underground symbol is everywhere. This version is at Arnos Grove, Piccadilly Line.

Cockfosters is due north of central London, but the Piccadilly sets off in a direction almost due east from the terminus before heading south. However, in Underground parlance this is called westbound! This follows a requirement that lines need to be referred to consistently throughout their length, and the main focus of the Piccadilly is certainly east/west.

Cockfosters is a four-platform station with three tracks; the depot occupies the eastbound side of the line from here to Oakwood.

Southgate station, well situated at the middle of the shopping centre, is in a short 850m tunnel; daylight at the end of the tunnel can be seen from the westbound platform. Arnos Grove, again three tracks and four platform faces, is designed to allow trains to terminate here; there are also some sidings.

The Piccadilly then enters bored tube tunnels, from which it does not emerge again until Barons Court. A turnback siding is provided for eastbound trains at Wood Green, while at Finsbury Park there are track connections with the Victoria Line for stock movement purposes. Cross-platform facilities are available for passengers. York Road is one of the several closed stations on the Piccadilly Line.

At King's Cross St Pancras there is a connection to the Northern Line, again for stock purposes, plus a trailing crossover. Close spacing of stations reaches the system's ultimate between Covent Garden and Leicester Square: only 0.26km. At Down Street, now closed, there is another turnback siding, this time for westbound trains. Almost without exception, the stations have island platforms. Brompton Road, west of Knightsbridge, is also closed.

The line rises to the surface at Barons Court, where it takes up a position between the District Line tracks; this continues for over 5km. There are connections from and to the District, plus a central siding which can be accessed from either direction. After the recently rebuilt Hammersmith, the Piccadilly runs fast to Acton Town with a running time of 5min as against the 8min for the District with four intermediate station calls. In any event, there is no eastbound fast line platform at Stamford Brook, and in neither direction at Chiswick Park. The limited facility now available at Acton Works is passed on the south side of the line.

At the four-platformed Acton Town, the facilities can fairly be described as copious. Piccadilly trains can use either platform. From here, the preponderance of service is to Heathrow. While the Piccadilly has the use of both westbound tracks beyond Acton Town to Northfields, the local line is accessed only from Platform 1. The eastbound local line for many years saw use only as a test track.

Four tracking ends at Northfields, where westbound trains dive under the depot access road. The Piccadilly skirts the north side of the depot, and there are further

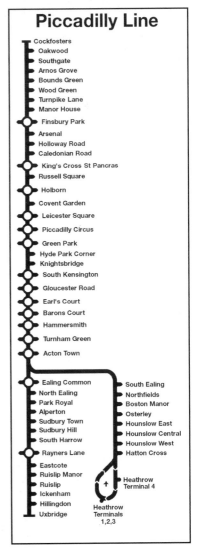

Piccadilly Line

- Cockfosters
- Oakwood
- Southgate
- Arnos Grove
- Bounds Green
- Wood Green
- Turnpike Lane
- Manor House
- Finsbury Park
- Arsenal
- Holloway Road
- Caledonian Road
- King's Cross St Pancras
- Russell Square
- Holborn
- Covent Garden
- Leicester Square
- Piccadilly Circus
- Green Park
- Hyde Park Corner
- Knightsbridge
- South Kensington
- Gloucester Road
- Earl's Court
- Barons Court
- Hammersmith
- Turnham Green
- Acton Town

- Ealing Common
- North Ealing
- Park Royal
- Alperton
- Sudbury Town
- Sudbury Hill
- South Harrow
- Rayners Lane
- Eastcote
- Ruislip Manor
- Ruislip
- Ickenham
- Hillingdon
- Uxbridge

- South Ealing
- Northfields
- Boston Manor
- Osterley
- Hounslow East
- Hounslow Central
- Hounslow West
- Hatton Cross
- Heathrow Terminal 4
- Heathrow Terminals 1,2,3

Above: **A Piccadilly Line train of 1973 stock leaves Hillingdon eastbound across the new bridge over the A40 to Oxford and Birmingham.**

connections at Boston Manor. At Hounslow West, the former terminus, the station is underground. For a short section the line rises again to the surface, to cross the River Crane. At Hatton Cross, trains take the single-line loop on the left to Heathrow Terminal 4 then on to Heathrow Terminals 1, 2 and 3. The former terminus has two platforms with a scissors crossover at the eastern end. Trains nominally terminate here (in either platform) with a stand of around 6min for recovery. They then return direct to Hatton Cross.

The railway west of Acton Town was very much dominated by the District, whose trains continued to run to Hounslow West until 1964. Northwards from Acton Town, the District's Ealing Broadway service shares the same tracks to Ealing Common (actually, until Hanger Lane Junction), after which the Piccadilly has sole use of the former District tracks to Rayners Lane. There are car

Above: **A concentration of infrastructure surrounds the Piccadilly Line trains at the west end of Acton Town. The D stock trains are in Ealing Common depot.**

stabling sidings at South Harrow. All the stations on this stretch have side platforms.

Rayners Lane, for long the terminus of most Piccadilly services, now sees Piccadilly Line trains continue over Metropolitan metals to Uxbridge.

Capacity is a Piccadilly Line problem, and efforts which have been made to speed loading and unloading at stations include recorded announcements. But station platforms are often less capacious than they might be. Failure to encourage passengers to move down the platform can mean that they choose not to take the next arriving train because it is full; which it may be where they are standing, but not necessarily at all points in the train. In vain do staff implore them to move along; the only short term answer is to close the platform gates until the crowds have cleared.

The Piccadilly is a busy railway and in 1995 had an originating traffic of 350,000 on an average weekday, or 13.9% of the Underground network total. But it also had the largest number of interchanging passengers, at 165,000. Daily usage was thus about 515,000 in total.

The busiest section in the peak three hours is Gloucester Road to South Kensington with 29,100 passengers, and the all day total for the section with the heaviest load is 93,600 from Hyde Park Corner to Green Park.

Apart from the Metropolitan, which specialises in longer distance journeys, the Piccadilly has the greatest average passenger journey distance at 9km. Overseas visitors also make up 15% of its total traffic, more than any other line. While both may in part be directly attributable to the Piccadilly's serving Heathrow, it also links hotel areas with the West End.

Piccadilly stations also include some with much bus feeder traffic. These include Manor House where 40% arrive by bus, which is a higher proportion than any other station, and both Wood Green and Hounslow East exceed 30%. Car-borne traffic is also a substantial source, with 40% or more passengers arriving by car at Arnos Grove, Hatton Cross and Osterley. National Railways' stations directly served are King's Cross, St Pancras and Finsbury Park.

Green Park is one of the busiest stations on the Piccadilly, with 41.3 million annual users in 1995. Of these, nearly half at 19.7 million were interchanging between the three lines here. The other 21.6 million passengers relate to the entrance/exit counts.

All Piccadilly Line services are provided by the six-car trains of 1973 stock. A total of 76 trains is required for the maximum service on Mondays to Fridays, reducing

to 66 on both Saturdays and Sundays. Other than the Victoria Line with Automatic Train Operation, the Piccadilly was the first tube line to change to One Person Operation in 1987.

The Line management team is located near South Kensington station.

Victoria Line

The origins of the Victoria Line can be traced back to before World War 2, but it came to more prominence subsequently. Building it for surface stock was considered, but this would have doubled the cost and severely constrained cross-platform interchange possibilities. Eventually, authorisation was obtained, and the line opening dates are shown below. The Victoria Line is 21.28km long and serves 16 stations between Walthamstow and Brixton.

1968   Walthamstow Central-Warren Street
1969   Warren Street-Victoria
1971   Victoria-Brixton

The whole line is underground from the passenger's point of view. In reality, the line depot is on the surface at Northumberland Park alongside the Railtrack Lea Valley line; access is from Seven Sisters.

From north to south, the line starts underneath Walthamstow Central Railtrack station in a standard island platform layout. A scissors crossover follows.

A three-platform Seven Sisters allows northbound trains to terminate in the centre Platform 4, but from this point they cannot directly travel southbound, for which they must shunt to Platform 5. They can also proceed to Northumberland Park depot, an option used for staff purposes. It may be added that Platforms 1 and 2 are those of the Railtrack station upstairs.

Cross-platform facilities are available at Finsbury Park with the Piccadilly and at Highbury & Islington with West Anglia Great Northern. King's Cross St Pancras has a turnback siding for northbound trains. For this section and as far as Warren Street (inclusive), right-hand running is used. The purpose was to maximise the interchange benefits at Euston, so that southbound Northern Line passengers from the High Barnet/Edgware direction have cross-platform interchange to take them to Oxford Circus and Victoria. The equivalent arrangement applies in the reverse direction.

Bakerloo Line passengers benefit from same-level interchange at Oxford Circus. There are trailing crossovers at Warren Street and Victoria, but the latter has two sidings south of the station platforms for terminating southbound trains. Stockwell also has a Northern Line cross-platform arrangement.

Pimlico station is the only one on the line with no rail interchange of any description.

The line terminates at Brixton in an arrangement similar to Walthamstow Central. In both cases, trains can be stabled in the over-run tunnels.

The line has been equipped with Automatic Train Operation from new, and has always been One Person Operated.

Now a quarter of a century old, renewals are becoming necessary. Some impact has been made on the rolling stock requirements by the conversion of 1972 MkI stock from the Northern Line, but this is only an interim approach. Should the line be extended south from Brixton, and if so, where to? On the surface or in tunnel? How would that compare with extending the Northern from Kennington or the Bakerloo from Elephant? Or, indeed, the dreaded do-nothing situation?

Any proposed actions must take line capacity into account; there is little point in adding to a facility if the

46

Above and below: A curious juxtaposition of signs greets the traveller arriving by North London Railways at Blackhorse Road. The Underground is upstairs, but on the way out (above), while the LUL station name display thanks one for travelling by an organisation defunct now for over three years (below). Photographed on 24 April 1997.

passenger numbers would just swamp the line. The aim is to make the Victoria Line a 90sec railway, at 40tph. Brixton is a bottleneck at present, albeit that stepping back of train crews allows a 2min turnround. A loop, with or without a station at Herne Hill, is one possibility. Another is a three-platform terminus.

Meanwhile, the Channel Tunnel Rail Link to St Pancras continues to make progress.

The Victoria Line originating passenger numbers are 290,000 per weekday, 11.5% of Underground carryings. Additional interchanging passengers add a further 150,000, giving a total of 440,000.

The busiest section of the line throughout the day is that from Victoria to Green Park, with 38,300 in the morning peak and 109,000 overall. Victoria is the busiest of all London Underground stations, with 66.2 million passengers passing through the barriers in the course of a year. With another 18 million changing between Underground lines, this gives the top annual usage of 84.2 million. This makes Victoria LUL station busier than all the London airports combined. Oxford Circus is a close second and King's Cross St Pancras third.

The average passenger journey length, at 8km, is among the highest. National Railways' interchanges take place at 11 of the 16 stations, and other Underground lines at eight of them. In all, 40% of Brixton passengers arrive by bus, and 30% of those joining at Walthamstow; 50% of both Tottenham Hale's and Victoria's passengers arrive by National Railways. Overall, people's methods of getting to the Victoria Line divide as 21% national railways, 12% bus, 4% car and the rest walk.

Services are provided by the eight-car trains of 1967 stock. A total of 37 trains is required for the maximum service on Mondays to Fridays, reducing to 25 on Saturdays and also on Sundays.

The Line management team is located at Oxford Circus.

Waterloo & City Line

The Waterloo & City Line opened in 1898. It was built by an associated company of the London & South Western

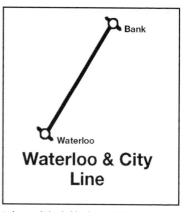

Waterloo & City Line

Railway, and absorbed by them in 1907. The purpose of the line was to convey L&SWR passengers to the City, from which Waterloo was relatively remote. Traffic has always been highly peaked. This was London's second tube railway, but not part of what became the Underground.

The line is 2.37km long and has stations at Waterloo and Bank only. It was transferred from the British Railways Board to London Underground Ltd on 1 April

Below: **The Waterloo & City trains look very smart, but not in anything which remotely could be called London Underground corporate livery. This train of 1992/Class 482 stock has just arrived.**

Above: **The business area of Waterloo as seen from the end of the arrival platform. A train of 1992 stock is approaching the departure platform.**

1994. The line is completely underground, other than the rolling stock access area.

The sidings and maintenance facility are at Waterloo, where the station has two side platforms, Nos 25 (eastbound) and 26 (westbound). Trains reverse at Waterloo via the depot area. The twin tubes pass under the Thames and a scissors crossover protects the entrance to Bank station. The platforms here are numbered 7 and 8.

About 55,000 passengers per day on Mondays to Fridays use the line for the 4min journey. The morning peak flow is from Waterloo to Bank and accounts for about 15,000 passengers.

Services are operated by slightly modified 1992 tube stock, of which there are 20 cars. The maximum service requirement on Mondays to Fridays is four sets, and two sets on Saturdays. All trains are made up of four cars. There is no Sunday service.

The Waterloo & City Line is managed by the Central Line team of London Underground.

In total, therefore, assuming operation of the East London Line and a Bakerloo service to Elephant, the maximum passenger stock requirements in May 1997 were as shown in the table on page 50.

From the table can be seen the present use of those valuable assets. Interestingly, the total surface fleets account for something just under one-third of the overall rolling stock requirement.

The maximum Saturday train requirement is 75% of the maximum on Mondays to Fridays, and on Sundays 65% of the Mondays to Fridays total. While these figures do not differentiate by time of day, they do indicate that weekend service levels are nowadays relatively generous compared with the Mondays to Fridays totals.

The rolling stock types are discussed in the next section.

Rolling stock fleets committed for maximum service, by day of week

Stock type	Mon-Fri trains	Mon-Fri cars	Sat trains	Sat cars	Sun trains	Sun cars
A	47	352	35	256	26	188
C	41	246	35	210	32	192
D	66	396	51	306	48	288
Total surface	154	994	121	772	106	668
1959/62/72 MkI	84	588	59	413	46	322
1967	37	296	25	200	25	200
1972 MkII	31	217	26	182	20	140
1973	76	456	66	396	66	396
1983	24	144	18	108	15	90
1992	76	592	47	368	38	304
Total tube	328	2,293	241	1,667	210	1,452
Grand total	482	3,287	362	2,439	316	2,120

Below: Lambeth North is a well-preserved version of the Yerkes tube station platforms; this is the southbound line, looking towards Elephant & Castle.

5
THE UNDERGROUND TRAIN

The surface and the tube lines each have their own type of rolling stock.

In London, the City & South London Railway running tunnels on the original section as built were a mere 10ft 2in (3.1m) in diameter, and very restrictive as a result. Later lines saw the internal tunnel diameters rise to 3.6m and then 3.8m with the Victoria Line.

Each of the tube railways has a different history and trains are not fully interchangeable between them. Besides tunnel diameters, another physical feature to be considered is the horizontal curvature, which results in throwover at the outer ends of the cars and at the car centre on the inside of the curve. Such problems are magnified in station platforms, though here the principal difficulty is the gap which opens up between the train doors and the platform edge. Line curvature is an effective limit on individual car length.

Platform length is another limitation on the number of cars of which a train is comprised, on the basis that trains must be fully accommodated with all doors available for public use in each platform. Again, there are differences between lines, while the Northern is notorious for the variations to be found within it.

Total line capacity is a function of the capacity of each train, multiplied by the maximum service frequency attainable. Traffic levels do of course vary during the course of the day and on different days of the week, but there are also changes over time. These may be due to matters as diverse as the state of the economy, changes in service quality, fare levels and public perceptions. The table overleaf illustrates this.

Below: **Platform curvature can be a decided problem, since it accentuates the car to platform gap. It also limits the driver's visibility of the train doors, making the use of multiple cctv cameras essential. These are the District platforms at Victoria. A C stock train is arriving on an inner rail Circle Line train.**

Passenger journeys by London Underground, selected years

Year	Total journeys (millions)	As index, 1972=100
1972	655	100
1982	498	76
1988/89	815	124
1992/93	728	111
1996/97	772	118

With such variations, it is difficult to plan adequately for the business's asset needs when those costly pieces of equipment may last for up to 40 years. While some flexibility can be built into a programme of mid-life refurbishment, an example being the new seating layouts which have been introduced on a number of stock types in recent times, there are practical limits to the changes which can be considered. Altering vehicle length or door positions would both be too prohibitively costly to be considered. The result is the inevitable compromise, albeit with the benefit of many years of experience as a guide.

The capacity of an individual train is determined by a number of factors. These include:

■ the length of the train, as determined by the number of cars;
■ the dimensions of each car, given also that the fewer the number of cars, the less room is consumed by the space between adjacent cars, and that empty cabs are effectively wasted space;
■ the door layout, whether single of double leaf, and door width; and
■ the internal layout, especially the ratio of seating to

Above: A 1973 stock train arrives at Ealing Common with a Rayners Lane to Arnos Grove service. The compromise height of the platform, which sees also the District Line's Ealing Broadway service, is noticeable for the step down into the tube stock.

Below: The 1992 tube stock has the centre seats set back in the ends of the cars, to maximise the amount of standing room available, as shown in this Driving Motor car.

standing capacity and the availability and positioning of grab-poles and handrails.

The real standing capacity is a matter of some debate. A calculation can be made based on the floor area occupied by each individual, but few wish to stand in that close proximity to each other. Furthermore, if they do so, the time taken to load and unload at stations gets progressively longer. This slows down the service and ultimately actually reduces total line capacity, since the minimum headway achievable lengthens. On the other hand, the maximum possible load needs to be known, to ensure the structural integrity of the vehicle under all possible circumstances and in the calculation of the braking power needed.

These matters are discussed in relation to each car type, or group of car types.

London Underground surface stock is identified by a letter, to which may be added a number for batch identification. This number is nominally the last two digits of the year of construction, though this may be somewhat approximate. Tube car types are identified by the year in which they were constructed; as with the surface stock, the year may not always coincide with reality. However, the important element is that each type

of stock should be capable of being distinguished separately.

There are essentially four types of car, though no types of stock include all car types:

■ Driving Motor (DM), with traction motors and driver's cab;

■ Non-Driving Motor (NDM), with traction motors but no cab;

■ Uncoupling Non-Driving Motor (UNDM), with traction motors and no cab, but with a control panel to allow uncoupling and shunting of a unit, while not occupying the space taken by a full cab; and

■ Trailer (T), no motors, no cab.

Most sets of cars are also distinguished by being either 'A' end or 'D' end; coupling can only be from 'A' to 'D', unless the electrical and air connections are reversible. Particular problems arise where trains can be turned in service.

An example of this is the Hainault loop on the Central Line. But rolling stock on the Circle, Hammersmith & City, Metropolitan, Northern and Piccadilly lines can also become turned. The effect is minimal if the train is completely reversible as with the C stock where all units have operative driving cabs, but is severe on the

Below: The Singapore Metro really shows what can be achieved in trains which are much wider than found in Britain, and also where the line curvature is such that wide gangways can be provided between vehicles. Again, all seating is longitudinal.

Above: The diminutive size of tube stock, in this case unrefurbished Victoria Line 1967 stock DM No 3177, is most noticeable when compared with the generous dimensions of the trains of the Singapore Mass Transit Railway.

Northern Line where units can only be coupled to other units the same way round and only half of the driving cabs can be used at the outer ends of trains.

The Northern has the added problem that the varied stock fleet tends to result in a larger spares stockholding than if the fleet were homogeneous.

On London Underground, train lengths vary between four cars (found nowadays only on the East London, Waterloo & City and on the Chesham branch of the Metropolitan); six cars (District, Circle, Hammersmith & City, Jubilee, Piccadilly); seven cars (Bakerloo, Northern); and eight cars (Central, Metropolitan, Victoria).

The introduction of 1995 stock for the Northern results in six-car trains for that line.

While it is in theory possible to make up a train of any number of cars, it is highly desirable to enable it to be split down into two or more sub-units of equal size for maintenance and other purposes. This much simplifies remarshalling; two four-car units are of little use if one is trying to make up a train of seven cars.

The distinction between the types of line and the rolling stock which runs upon them is not absolute. Tube-dimensioned trains can be run extensively on the surface lines if required, though the reverse is obviously

impractical. All day operation over the same metals is limited to the Piccadilly and Metropolitan lines between Rayners Lane and Uxbridge and the Piccadilly and District lines between Acton Town and Ealing Common. Other limited movements may take place where lines run in parallel, such as between the Jubilee and Metropolitan lines on the section from Finchley Road to Wembley Park.

There is also the difficulty of any line-specific equipment which may be required. This affects engineering trains in particular. Automatic Train Operation and lack of train stops on the Victoria Line is an example, plus any physical limitations.

Surface Stock
A stock

The Metropolitan A60 stock was built by Cravens of Sheffield for the extension of electrification and selective four-tracking to Amersham. This scheme was aborted due to World War 2, but was finally completed in 1962. Amersham is 43km from central London. With a journey time of an hour to the City, it was felt that something a little bit special was needed for the Metropolitan's discerning customers. The A stock supplanted compartment stock with slam doors. A

Above: The A stock was a successful build of the early 1960s, to the extent that these trains as refurbished are expected to last until well into the 21st century. An Uxbridge service arrives at Farringdon in the evening peak.

Below: The London Underground corporate livery evolved through a number of trial applications, albeit using the same colours. This version had blue upper panels and light grey lower ones; the A stock train is on the East London Line, emerging from the tunnel at Surrey Quays. It is bound for New Cross.

further build, now A62 stock, was destined for the Uxbridge line; in practice both types are almost identical and are used as such.

The original order was for 62 A60 four-car units and 54 A62 units, of which nearly all survive. These trains are used on the Metropolitan Line as eight-car formations, with a four-car formation for the Chesham branch shuttle. They are also used as four-car units on the East London Line. The trains have been converted for One Person Operation (OPO), and are being refurbished by ADtranz at Derby in a programme due to be completed in 1997.

Driving Motors have two pairs of double doors per side and one single leaf door at the end; Trailers have three pairs of double leaf doors. Seating is all transverse in a three/gangway/two (3+2) layout.

The formation of an eight-car train is DM-T-T-DM+DM-T-T-DM, dimensions as follows:

Length per car	16.17m
Width per car	2.95m
Height	3.89m
Unladen weight	21.8-32.1 tonnes
Total seating capacity, 8 cars	448
Total standing capacity, 8 cars	976
Total train capacity, 8 cars	1,424

The Metropolitan Line's main depot is at Neasden, with additional facilities for stabling trains at Uxbridge, Rickmansworth and Wembley Park.

C stock

The Circle and the Hammersmith & City lines are both busy inner area services for which a high density design was eminently suitable. The C69 stock, as it became, was built by Metro-Cammell of Birmingham, replacing the CO/CP stock of the 1930s. These latter cars were transferred to the District Line.

A total of 212 new C stock cars were ordered, to make up 35 six-car trains, plus one spare two-car unit. The base element of a two-car unit consists of a Driving Motor car and a Trailer; three such sets make up a complete train. These trains are always used as six-car formations.

A subsequent order for more of the same produced a second batch, the C77 cars. This comprised 67 cars, including one DM to replace a C69 DM which was destroyed in a bomb incident at West Ham in 1976. The 11 new trains were for the Edgware Road-Wimbledon service of the District Line, the CO/CP stock having finally been retired. For this work, the internal layout of the C stock (see opposite) is perhaps a little less suitable, since the traffic is more suburban in nature. However, the choice was dictated by the short platforms of the western part of the Circle Line which make the subsequent D stock trains too long for this work.

The trains have been converted for One Person Operation (OPO), and were refurbished by RFS Industries in Doncaster between 1991 and 1994.

All C stock cars have the unique feature (for London Underground) of four pairs of double doors on each side.

Above: A New Cross Gate train formed of D stock (or D78 stock if you prefer), again arriving at Surrey Quays but en route for New Cross Gate.

Below left: A C stock train arrives at Fulham Broadway with an Edgware Road-Wimbledon District Line service in June 1997.

Seating, originally transverse with a 2+2 arrangement, except at the outer ends of each car where longitudinal seats were provided, was converted to longitudinal throughout on refurbishment. This was achieved by placing a row of four seats between each double door pair, with two seats at the end as before. The total seating capacity was unchanged.

Another change introduced at the same time was the provision of windows in the ends of all cars which did not also contain a driving cab. This was to enhance perceptions of personal security.

Unusually, the passenger saloons of DMs and Trailers are identical in length and layout; the driving cab is added on as an extra module.

The formation of a six-car train is DM-T+DM-T+T-DM, dimensions as follows:

Length per car DM	16.03m
Length per car T	14.94m
Width per car	2.92m
Height	3.68m
Unladen weight	20.5-32.2 tonnes
Total seating capacity, 6 cars	192
Total standing capacity, 6 cars	1,080
Total train capacity, 6 cars	1,272

The C stock trains are allocated to Hammersmith and Neasden depots, with additional siding space at Parsons Green and at Triangle Sidings, south of High Street Kensington.

D stock

The District Line's D stock was built by Metro-Cammell and entered service between 1979 and 1983. It replaced the rather splendid R stock, constructed over the years from 1938, with the last few dating from 1959. The R stock had latterly been running as seven-car formations, but the opportunity was taken to create the same train length of 100m with six instead of seven cars.

The D stock order was sufficient to form 75 six-car trains, each of which was made up of 2x3-car units. The order was made up of 65 'A' or 'D' end units, both of which are formed of Driving Motor, Trailer and Uncoupling Non-Driving Motor car. In addition, there are 20 units where a second Driving Motor replaces the UNDM. These dual-ended units can be used to substitute for either 'A' or 'D' units if required so to do.

The D stock trains have always operated as six-car trains apart from a short sojourn on the East London Line as three-car units in 1985-7, when double-ended trains were used for this purpose.

For the first time with surface stock, the doors consist of four pairs of single leaf doors per vehicle side. These doors are also passenger operated. Seating is mostly longitudinal, with a double pair of 2+2 transverse seats in the centre of each car.

The formation of a six-car train is DM-T-UNDM+UNDM-T-DM. A DM may substitute for one of the UNDMs.

Dimensions are as follows:

Length per car	18.13-18.37m
Width per car	2.85m
Height	3.62m
Unladen weight	18.7-27.9 tonnes
Total seating capacity 6 cars	280
Total standing capacity, 6 cars	1,092
Total train capacity, 6 cars	1,372

The District Line's depots are at Upminster and Ealing Common, with additional siding space at Parsons Green and Barking.

Tube Stock
1959/62 stock

The 1959 and 1962 tube stocks were originally built for the Piccadilly Line (as seven-car trains) and Central Line (as eight-car trains) respectively. All the 1,256 cars were built by Metro-Cammell, with a little help for 1962 stock trailers from British Railways' Derby works, as it then was. In both cases, these new trains replaced fleets of (mostly) pre-1938 or Standard stock.

The Heathrow extension of the Piccadilly Line dictated the need for new stock there, and this prompted a wholesale cascade of the 1959 trains to the Northern. Some also saw service on the Bakerloo. On the Northern they joined the 1972 MkI fleet, of which more anon.

Further stock was released from Central Line duties with the commissioning of the 1992 stock there.

Until such time as all the 1995 stock built for the Northern Line has entered service, substantial numbers of the 1959/62 fleets will remain in use there.

The existing fleet is of strictly traditional design. The visual differences compared with their 1938 stock predecessors are mainly the unpainted aluminium body shells replacing painted steel, fluorescent lighting, roller blind destination indicators, and a slightly modified internal seating arrangement. Other changes include the provision of rubber suspension and external door indicator lights for the benefit of the guard. These trains have always been, and remain, crew operated. Consequently, provision for the guard and the door

Left: The interior of 1959 stock appears decidedly homely, especially when in clean condition as here, at **Mill Hill East**.

Opposite: A train of 1959 stock stands inside Morden Northern Line depot, in decidedly clean condition.

Below: 1967 stock Driving Motor No 3153 at Northumberland Park depot.

controls may be found in the leading end of the last vehicle in each train.

The present formation of all trains to meet the seven-car Northern Line requirement is Driving Motor, Trailer, Non-Driving Motor and Driving Motor, plus two more Driving Motors with a Trailer in between.

All cars have two pairs of double doors on each side and a single door at the end without a cab (DMs) or at each end (NDM, T). Seating is longitudinal except in the centre sections, where two pairs of transverse 2+2 seats form seating bays.

No refurbishment has been carried out on the 1959/62 stock, other than experimentally.

The formation of a seven-car train is DM-T-NDM-DM+DM-T-DM, dimensions as follows:

Length per car DM	16.15m
Length per car NDM, T	14.94m

Width per car	2.60m
Height	2.88m
Unladen weight	21.0-27.0 tonnes
Total seating capacity, 7 cars	288
Total standing capacity, 7 cars	876
Total train capacity, 7 cars	1,164

The 1959/62 stock trains are allocated to the main depots at Golders Green and Morden, with additional train stabling space at Highgate, Edgware and High Barnet.

1967 stock

The Victoria Line was equipped with Automatic Train Operation (ATO) from its opening in 1968 onwards. An entirely new fleet of trains was required, which was built by Metro-Cammell. The original order was for 244 vehicles, later expanded by a further 72 vehicles when the Brixton extension was authorised. The total order

Above: A line-up of 1967, 1959 and 1972 MkI stock at Morden depot on 3 November 1990 illustrates their considerably different profiles. In retrospect, the designs are separated by only about 10 years.

was thus for 316 vehicles, or 39.5 trains, each of eight cars.

The 1967 stock trains are made up of two four-car units. Each of these consists of two Driving Motors and two intermediate trailers. There are equal numbers of 'A' end and 'D' end units.

The 1967 stock has always operated as eight-car trains on the Victoria Line, although a reduction to four-cars was made when they intermittently provided the Woodford-Hainault service on the Central Line when that section of line was ATO equipped.

Door and internal layout is very similar to that of the 1959/62 family of stock, apart from the 1967 trailers which have longitudinal seating throughout. The trains underwent mid-life refurbishment by Tickford Rail Ltd at Rosyth Dockyard between 1991 and 1995.

The formation of an eight-car train is DM-T-T-DM+DM-T-T-DM. The dimensions are:

Length per carDM	16.08m
Length per carT	15.98m
Width per car	2.64m
Height	2.87m
Unladen weight	20.6-30.9 tonnes
Total seating capacity, 8 cars	304
Total standing capacity, 8 cars	1,144
Total train capacity, 8 cars	1,448

The Victoria Line's depot is at Northumberland Park, with additional train stabling at Walthamstow Central and Brixton.

1972 stock

When additional tube rolling stock became a political imperative, the result was the ordering of further fleets from Metro-Cammell to the 1967 stock design but for crew operation. There were two batches.

The 1972 MkI fleet consisted of 30 seven-car trains for the Northern Line, made up of the traditional four-car and three-car formations with a UNDM substituting for the second Driving Motor in the three-car unit. The DM cars of course carried a guard's panel.

These trains have remained on the Northern since, until rolling stock shortages on the Victoria Line as a result of traffic growth prompted the search for additional trains. By confining the Driving Motors to the centre of an eight-car Victoria Line train, the technical work was minimised. A total of 5x4 car units and 4x3 car units from the 1972 MkI fleet, or 28 cars with four spares, was sufficient to raise the Victoria Line fleet from 39.5 to 43. Other cars were ceded to the Bakerloo Line.

Northern Line depots are as shown under the 1959/62 stock.

The 1972 MkII trains were immediately distinguishable by featuring red painted external doors and a prominent roundel on the bodyside. This fleet of 33 trains, again seven-cars, has operated successively on the Northern, the Jubilee when it was first opened, the Northern again, and is now on the Bakerloo. Provision was made with this stock for future conversion to ATO, but this was never carried out. However, it was altered for OPO.

Above: Two trains of 1972 MkI stock at Morden, the train on the left arriving on a service via Bank. The tunnel entrance can be seen in the background.

The 1972 MkII fleet underwent refurbishment by Tickford Rail between 1991 and 1995.

Bakerloo Line depots are at Stonebridge Park, Queen's Park and London Road (near Lambeth North station). There is additional siding space at Elephant & Castle.

Dimensions of the 1972 stock are, by definition, very similar to the 1967 cars, qv. However, train capacity for a MkII stock train is shown below. That for MkI stock is a little less, due to the space taken up by the guard.

Total seating capacity, 7 cars	264
Total standing capacity, 7 cars	1,014
Total train capacity, 7 cars	1,278

Above: A 1972 MkII train approaches Willesden Junction on a train for Elephant & Castle on 21 March 1990. This is Railtrack territory, the line being used also by the Watford-Euston dc services of North London Railways. It also represents the only means by which Bakerloo trains can reach their Stonebridge Park depot.

Above: The refurbished 1973 stock livery is closer to the newer 1995/6 stocks. A train arrives from Uxbridge at the rebuilt Hillingdon station on 15 March 1997.

1973 stock

The 1973 stock for the Piccadilly Line was the first where a concerted move was made towards longer cars and a reduction of the seven-car requirement to six-cars. It may be added that this also cuts the number of bodies and bogies to be built, and is in itself an economy measure whatever other benefits may accrue.

The length of a 1973 stock train is around 5m less than that of its 1959 predecessor, but trains were an uncomfortably tight fit to the platforms at some stations.

A prime requirement for the new design was to accommodate luggage for airport passengers as best it could; as built, the 1973 stock had an enlarged standback provided inside the doorways for this purpose. In practice, few used it, preferring to inflict discomfort on themselves and others rather than move any distance away from their luggage.

A fleet of 87.5 six-car trains was supplied by Metro-Cammell. Most of the three-car sets are made up of a Driving Motor, a central Trailer and a UNDM; 21 are cabbed at both ends in a DM-T-DM formation for flexibility. When built and indeed until 1994 when the service was withdrawn, one double-cabbed unit was required for the Aldwych shuttle. There have never been any other three-car set workings.

The guard was accommodated in the rear cab, in common with many other rolling stock types. This

feature was abandoned when OPO was introduced.

The 1973 stock features two pairs of double doors on each body side, plus single doors at the car ends except where these are adjacent to the driver's cab. Internally, the cars have longitudinal seating throughout post-refurbishment, a task being carried out by Bombardier Prorail, in a programme due to be completed in 1999. This also features a luggage bay, created by the removal of seats in the central section of each car, albeit that perch seats are provided for use when the space is not being used for luggage. There are further perch seats at the car ends.

The usual formation of a six-car train is DM-T-UNDM+UNDM-T-DM. Principal details for refurbished trains are:

Length per car DM	17.676m
Length per car UNDM, T	17.473m
Width per car	2.629m
Height	2.880m
Unladen weight	18.5-27.6 tonnes
Total seating capacity, 6 cars	228, plus 44 perch seats
Total standing capacity, 6 cars	966
Total train capacity, 6 cars	1,238

Above right: Inside the cab of a 1983 stock Jubilee Line train.

Above left: Time is running out for the 1983 stock on the Jubilee Line. On a bright 28 December 1986, a train for Charing Cross arrives at Neasden. The bridge in the background carries the North Circular Road.

The Piccadilly Line's main depots are at Northfields and Cockfosters, with additional siding space at South Harrow, Acton Town and Arnos Grove.

1983 stock

The 1983 tube stock was the response to the need for additional trains for the separation of the Jubilee Line from the Bakerloo in 1979 and its extension over new construction from Baker Street to Bond Street, Green Park and Charing Cross. Originally conceived as then continuing towards the City, Jubilee Line plans were eventually shelved and the rolling stock order finalised at 15 trains in what was then a falling market. As usual, the trains were supplied by Metro-Cammell.

With at least a passing resemblance to the surface D stock for the District Line, the six-car trains consist of 2x3-car units, each made up of a Driving Motor, Trailer and another Driving Motor. Car lengths were again extended, to make them slightly longer than the 1973 stock.

For the first time in recent years on tube stock, passenger door opening by push buttons was provided, while the doors themselves, four per vehicle side on the trailers but three on the DMs, were of single leaf only. The internal layout was mostly longitudinal seating, but two pairs of 2+2 transverse seats form a bay in the middle of each car. Coupled with a minimal standback inside the doors, these trains have proved slow to load and unload.

These were delivered between 1983 and 1985, but traffic growth had already led to thoughts of restoring the order to something nearer the volume originally intended. The result was the construction of 16.5 more six-car trains, known as Batch II, delivered in 1987/8. Minor differences only were apparent, such as replacing the shielded fluorescent lighting with standard fittings. The arrival of the Batch II sets coincided with the conversion of the Jubilee Line to OPO.

The formation of a six-car train is DM-T-DM+DM-T-DM, dimensions as follows:

Length per car DM	17.68m
Length per car T	17.73m
Width per car	2.63m
Height	2.88m
Unladen weight	20.4-26.3 tonnes
Total seating capacity, 6 cars	288
Total standing capacity, 6 cars	878
Total train capacity, 6 cars	1,166

The Jubilee Line's depot is at Neasden, with additional siding space at Stanmore.

The 1983 stock on the Jubilee Line is being replaced by the 1996 stock, presently in course of delivery. The single doors of the 1983 stock were judged to be a serious inhibition to achieving acceptable boarding and alighting times on the Jubilee Line Extension, and their replacement avoids the problems of a mixed fleet on the line.

It is anticipated that at least some of the 1983 stock will eventually find a use on the Piccadilly Line; certainly, car length would produce difficulties on some lines. Scrapping may be a more realistic alternative.

1992 stock

The 1992 tube stock was built by ADtranz and was the outcome of the trials of three prototype four-car trains of 1986 tube stock: the Red train A, the Blue train B, and the Green train C. These were built by Metro-Cammell; what was then BREL Derby; and again Metro-Cammell. All were substantially different, including the suppliers of traction equipment, the bogies, the brakes, the heating and ventilation systems, the interior layout and finish. The 1986 trains were later used experimentally in passenger service on the Jubilee Line.

The contract for the 85 eight-car Central Line trains was awarded to BREL's successor, ABB Transportation. A further order for 10 two-car units was added on, for the Waterloo & City Line stock replacement. At the time, this line was owned by the British Railways Board.

Trains were delivered from 1992 onwards, entering service from spring 1993. The body shells are made from welded extruded aluminium sections. The twin sliding doors, plus one at each end of each car, are wider than any used previously on tube stock. (Each door leaf is 832mm.) The doors are externally hung. In both respects the 1992 cars are very different from their most recent production predecessors of 1983 stock.

Traction equipment was supplied by ABB/Brush and bogies were from Kawasaki of Japan. The driver's controls comprise a fore-aft traction brake controller which is provided to the right of the driver's seat. In-cab closed circuit television is provided for platform observation, which eliminates the need for platform mirrors and monitors.

The car interiors have longitudinal seating only, with five per side in the centre bay and six per side in the ends. The centre two seats of each group of six are set back to give as much standing space as possible. Perch seats are also provided in the corners of all car ends without a cab, and there are also large windows in car ends for security. Both passenger door 'open' and 'close' buttons are provided. All side windows curve towards the roof, to make station names more visible to standing passengers.

The eight-car trains for the Central Line consist of 4x2-car semi-permanently coupled units, each made up variously from a Driving Motor and a Non-Driving Motor

Above: A train of 1992 stock arrives at Epping, a station which still very much shows its Great Eastern origins. The date is 29 September 1994, the last week of the branch thence to Ongar.

or pairs of Non-Driving Motors. All axles are motored for smooth and rapid acceleration. In each unit, both of the vehicles have traction equipment and an automatic coupler at the outer end, but only one has pick-up shoes so that its partner depends on it for electrical supplies. All of the Non-Driving Motors have shunting control cabinets at their outer ends. Each unit is fully reversible.

It follows that the formation of an eight-car train will vary, but typically might be DM-NDM+NDM-NDM+NDM-NDM+NDM-DM. The total number of Driving Motors is 175, but 170 are needed to provide a cab at each end of the 85 trains. Car dimensions are as follows in all cases:

Length per car	16.25m
Width per car	2.62m
Height	2.87m
Unladen weight	20.5-22.5 tonnes
Total seating capacity, 8 cars	272
Total standing capacity, 8 cars	1,380
Total train capacity, 8 cars	1,652

The Central Line's depots are Ruislip, White City and Hainault, with additional siding space at Woodford and Loughton. The Waterloo & City Line depot is at Waterloo.

1995 stock

GEC-Alsthom, who acquired Metro-Cammell of Birmingham in 1989, entered into a novel agreement with London Underground for the supply of 106 new trains for the Northern Line in spring 1995. The trains are generally similar to the 1996 stock which is preceding them into service, but the body shells are slightly more constrained to fit the tube gauge.

The trains themselves are of six cars, made up of two three-car units as follows: Driving Motor, Trailer and Non-Driving Motor. A complete train will thus be DM-T-UNDM+UNDM-T-DM. All have longitudinal seating only.

Length per car	17.77m
Width per car	2.63m
Height	2.875m
Total seating capacity, 6 cars	200 plus 20 perch seats and 48 tip-up seats. There are also 24 wheelchair spaces.

The supply contract is discussed in Chapter 9.

Above: **The new Northern Line 1995 stock from GEC-Alsthom; the first train to be delivered with Dm No 51501 nearest the camera is seen at Ruislip on 15 May 1997.**

Above: This view of the interior of DM No 51501 shows how seating has been cut back to make more space for standing passengers, wheelchairs and luggage.

Right: Front end of the 1996 Jubilee Line stock at Ruislip depot on 15 March 1997. This is Driving Motor No 96009.

Opposite top: The underside of 1996 stock DM No 96009 is still beautifully clean, as befits a new vehicle.

Opposite: 1996 Jubilee Line stock at Ruislip, with battery locomotive L50 in the foreground.

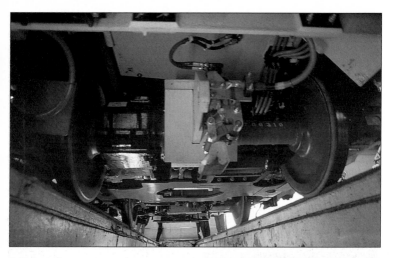

1996 stock

The fleet of 59 trains for the Jubilee Line features bays for shopping, pushchairs or the mobility impaired, profiled seats for comfort, forced-air ventilation, perch seats at the ends of the cars, 'next station' dot-matrix indicators and audio messages.

They are also self-diagnostic and require service at extended intervals only.

Each three-car unit is made up of a Driving Motor, a Trailer and a Non-Driving Motor. Two such units coupled together form a six-car train, whose make-up is thus DM-T-UNDM+UNDM-T-DM. It will be possible to add an additional Trailer in the future, should this be required for traffic reasons.

Internally, the trains are similar to those for the Northern Line, but additional perch seats replace the tip-up seats in the same numbers. There is capacity for 268 seated and a further 772 standing passengers, total 1,040.

GEC-Alsthom have a contract with London Underground to maintain the 1996 stock trains for 10 years. The deal includes financial penalties if the standards set by London Underground are not met. This does of course require enforceable and quantified definitions of words like reliability, availability and failures, while both parties need to keep records of what actually transpires.

The design target for the trains is 25,000km between failures, whereas the 1983 stock achieves less than 5,000km. GEC-Alsthom will take responsibility for:

- train cleaning
- train preparation for service
- day-to-day train maintenance, including materials
- stores management
- all component and sub-assembly failures
- premature obsolescence
- train-borne communication and signalling modules removal and replacement
- plant and equipment employed in train maintenance
- the security of Stratford Market depot.

London Underground remains responsible for the depot signalling, track and premises maintenance and contract management. Stratford Market succeeds Neasden as the principal line maintenance depot.

Engineering Fleet

TransPlant, the Engineers' Trains section, has bases at Lillie Bridge, Ruislip, Neasden and Ealing Common. These include both train operation and maintenance, and about 15 trains are run each night.

Such work is constrained by the limited time available for work to be carried out between last trains and early morning services (unless prolonged line closures are agreed), the equipment limitations of surface and tube gauge, and site access. Each working site must be declared safe after passage of the last service train; likewise, the site must be cleared and any testing completed before traction current can be restored. Cumulatively, these result in around 4-5hr being available for productive work to be carried out.

The principal motive power are the very costly battery locomotives, which move a variety of wagon types and cranes. There are self-propelled tamping machines and a weed-killing train.

Below: Old stager Metropolitan locomotive No 12 *Sarah Siddons* at Watford, having just run round a special train. The retention of *Sarah* is justified by the Director of Mechanical Engineering as a Brake Block Test Locomotive.

6

THE UNDERGROUND TODAY

Infrastructure

Without an adequate infrastructure, London Underground will never be able to offer a fast and reliable train service, with high ride quality, running at higher service frequencies and carrying increasing numbers of customers.

The operation of trains on the Underground is controlled by the signalling system, which works on the principle of not more than one train being permitted in each section of track (or block) at any one time. These blocks are monitored by track circuits which detect the presence of a train by means of a low voltage current between the running rails. The presence of a train causes a short circuit. London Underground has over 8,000 track circuits. Apart from the Victoria Line which is equipped with Automatic Train Operation, this system relies on signals which turn red as a train enters a block, together with train stops which raise a trackside arm to apply the brakes of any following train which attempts to pass that signal. The train stop lowers as the signal clears, when the first train moves to the next block. LUL has 3,440 train stops.

Train speeds are to a large extent controlled by the driver. The signalling is a significant factor in determining line capacity, the maximum frequency at which trains can be operated. Other factors include the flexibility of the track layout, the operation and position of junctions, and the length of time needed for the station stop. Around half of the signalling system is 20 years old or more.

The traditional signalling of fixed block, manual driving and based on track circuits limits service density,

particularly when other factors such as variations in driving techniques and physical line constraints are taken into account. Automatic train control, as being introduced on the Central Line, is designed to allow a service frequency of 33 trains per hour (tph).

In the longer term, moving block systems offer greater advances. The principle is that a safe distance is continuously maintained between any two trains such that the second train can always be brought to a halt before any impact. Moving block signalling is most easily provided using a transmission based system, with two-way communication between train-carried equipment and a trackside computer. The train detection offered by the track circuit is not required.

Significant improvements in service density are possible. The first manifestation on London Underground is the Jubilee Line, where Westinghouse Signals are providing a radio-based automatic train control system to allow the provision of a 36tph service, or a train every 100sec.

London Underground's 1,093km track, consisting of running rails and two conductor rails, is supported in the open and sub-surface sections by softwood (still much more numerous) or concrete sleepers set in limestone or granite ballast. Point and crossing work is supported by either hardwood or softwood sleepers, while in the tunnels hardwood sleepers concreted into the tunnel inverts are generally used.

The running rails are either bullhead (again, much in the majority) or flat-bottomed rails, secured by either chairs or base plates. To a considerable extent, LUL now uses 91.44m lengths of long-welded rail, tight-jointed up

Left: Weed-killer operations are the preserve of Motor Cars No L151/2, themselves derived from 1938 tube stock and pictured here at Ruislip.

Above: A diesel crane and jib carrier at Acton Works, 1983.

to 730m in length and provided with adjustment switches. Two types of conductor rail are used, flat-bottomed in open sections and square section in tunnels. They are mounted on porcelain insulators secured to the sleepers.

The track itself is the key issue and, throughout the system, track is scheduled to be replaced over the next decade. This is at the least a disruptive task, and it makes sense to undertake other related activities at the same time. The case is strengthened by the difficulties of obtaining adequate track possessions, to which reference has already been made.

The underlying problems concern matters such as the stability of embankments (as in the 1994 slip at Colindale, which required train service suspension for 15 days and cost £400,000 to rectify) or cuttings. These earthworks are becoming increasingly unserviceable, due to lack of past maintenance, age and inadequacies in the original work.

Another issue is inadequate track drainage. Drainage needs to be sustained, since water poses five main threats to the integrity of the Underground system:

- derailment resulting from displaced ballast;
- collision resulting from displaced track;
- suspension of service resulting from flooding;
- station closure resulting from flooding; and
- wet trackbeds resulting in deterioration of the formation.

Solutions include planned preventative maintenance, system redesign and refurbishment, or — unsatisfactorily — reacting to problems as they arise.

London's water table is rising following the reduction in manufacturing: at Trafalgar Square it is rising at the rate of 2.5m a year.

Abstraction of water is essential. The drainage problem, in two senses, will not go away! There are at present 700 drainage pumps.

Supporting structures also have their problems. Thus, the strength of many bridges is insufficient to carry the loads arising from the new track forms, while discontinuities caused by certain types of bridge deck lead to difficulties in maintaining ride quality and give high maintenance costs.

There are also 8km of urban viaducts, such as on the western end of the Hammersmith & City Line. Waterproofing of viaducts is needed in many areas, which necessitates track removal to expose the top of the structure. The collapse of a viaduct parapet at Ravenscourt Park caused serious service interruption.

Renovation of sub-surface tunnels is needed, while certain parts of tube tunnels also require renovation or alteration to deal with gauging problems, acid attack on cast tunnel linings as at Old Street, or tunnel protection works under the Thames (Bakerloo, East London and Northern Lines).

In addition, the provision of cable runs, whether for power supplies, communications or signalling, can all usefully be undertaken during a co-ordinated period of engineering possessions.

Even so, and assuming the practicalities of integrating such work can be mastered, adequate funding on a continuous basis is essential, and this is again not available. Work as described is essentially renewals investment, defined as 'programmed expenditure on existing infrastructure and buildings which represents like-for-like replacement or improvement, and alterations without improvements'. It does not include day-to-day maintenance nor, indeed, large scale capital projects such as the Jubilee Line Extension.

The backlog is likely again to grow, as the following examples (as at early 1997) show that:

■ Out of a total of 295 signalling installations, there are 32 in operation which are more than 45 years old, having been installed between 1940 and 1949.
■ Out of a total of 303 escalators, there are 27 in operation which are more than 45 years old, having been installed between 1932 and 1951. There are also 66 lifts of similar age.

There were also two network-wide power failures in 1996/7. London Underground has a peak demand for electricity during a severe winter of about 230MW. About 70% of the total needs to come from the power stations at Lots Road, Chelsea, and at Greenwich. The balance is obtained from the National Grid.

There are also 115 sub-stations.

As a guide to asset life, London Underground estimates the useful lives of its assets as follows, for depreciation purposes. That for rolling stock was increased from 40 years in 1996-7.

Rolling stock	up to 50 years
Escalators	up to 40 years
Lifts	40-75 years
Electricity supply	15-40 years
Other plant and equipment	up to 30 years

The Station

The train operator's view of a station is not that of the passenger. The operator wants to keep his costs to a minimum, allow for peak passenger volumes in the design of passages and platforms, provide adequate space for ticketing, and offer good visibility for staff, whether to supervise what is happening or to deter vandalism. Above all, he wants to keep things moving; the rate of platform clearance must be at least equal to the speed at which new passengers arrive on the platform. For that reason, crowd control measures are needed, using the Bostwick lattice gates or perhaps on occasion restricting station entry.

As to station design, side platforms keep flows of passengers separated by direction and minimise speed constraints associated with track curvature. Island platforms use only one set of facilities, whether they be escalators for access or the presence of staff.

The problems clearly multiply at interchange stations. Another consideration is changes in patronage over time. The Victoria Line was built with substandard platform widths as an economy measure, which reduced the volume of spoil to be removed. It shows. This may have helped to secure the line being built in the first place, but it is something which is not easily rectified at a later date.

Passenger needs centre on minimising walking distance and the time taken to access the platform, the provision of adequate circulating space, unambiguous direction finding, real time information systems (as in

Below: **The Unimog vehicle has the problem of not being relied upon to operate track circuits. However, with transmission-based signalling, this becomes somewhat academic. No GR5143 is seen here at Ruislip.**

the dot-matrix platform indicators) and a safe environment. New for London with the Jubilee Line Extension are the platform edge doors and the associated screens at the underground stations, and the public reaction will be of interest.

It was calculated long ago that two escalators could do the work of five lifts, so the lift was quickly supplanted. The escalator has the great advantage of offering a continuous service, which is not suspended in the sense of denying access if it cannot be operated for any reason. Escalators can also be used in the reverse direction. However, the escalator is less successful where distances are long (as with the 27.4m vertical rise at Angel), since it is relatively slow. Experimentation with speeds of up to 55m per minute has been carried out, but passengers do not feel secure and any overall time advantage is lost through hesitation on entry causing slow boarding speeds. There are also those who have difficulty in using any escalator.

The lift comes into its own at deep level stations, and is virtually a prerequisite for the mobility handicapped. In this context, it must be remembered that a lift from platform level to a sub-surface ticket hall does not solve the problem for the individual of reaching street level.

Other matters to be addressed include station ventilation. It may be noted that the platform edge doors on the Jubilee Line Extension are above train height but do not reach the ceiling. Station platforms may thus still be ventilated by the movement of the trains.

As many as 115 of London Underground's stations are deemed to come under the requirements of the Fire Precautions (Sub-Surface Railway Stations) Regulations 1989, made under Section 12 of the Fire Precautions Act 1971. All these stations are provided with comprehensive fire prevention and detection systems, and also with station radio and public address facilities.

The Ticketing System

Between 1987 and 1989, London Underground installed the Underground Ticketing System (UTS). This involved the modification of ticket offices and the installation of ticket issuing equipment at all LUL's stations, then 241 in total. All passenger-operated ticket machines are wall-mounted and are accessed from the rear for the purposes of cash clearance, ticket roll renewal and general maintenance.

There are three machine types:

■ The Ticket Office Machine, used by the ticket clerk.
■ The Few Fare Machine, used by the passenger, which can offer up to 10 different preset ticket types and accepts coins only.
■ The Multi Fare Machine, again used by the passenger, which can offer a wide range of ticket types and accepts notes up to £20 as well as coins.

Most tickets valid on LUL services are in the form of a card 87mm x 54mm, similar in size to a standard credit card. These feature a magnetic stripe along the centre of

Below: **Hillingdon station was reconstructed on a new site at the expense of the Department of Transport, to allow the A40 to be rebuilt on a new alignment. This included the provision of a new railway bridge, seen here being crossed by A stock from Uxbridge to Baker Street.**

Above right: **The barrier line for UTS gates at Edgware Road surface lines station.**

the ticket back and printed details of the issuing station, ticket type, validity, fare paid, date and time of issue on the face.

The Treasury limits the float for change that a ticket machine can carry to £50. Even so, this accounts for perhaps £75,000 in coins across the London Underground system.

Initially, ticket checking gates were installed at 63 stations in Zone 1. A computer centre provides a central collection point for ticket sales and performance data. An Operations Control Centre at Baker Street overviews the operation of all ticketing equipment. Subsequently, more stations have been gated.

Using the UTS system, the passenger is instructed to proceed as follows:

'Insert your ticket in the slot, retrieve it and the gate will open. If the value of travel on your ticket is used up at the end of your journey the gate will open but the machine will keep your ticket.' (Travelling in London, 1997)

The inward ticket gate reads and interprets a magnetically encoded ticket inserted with the code facing down, print facing upwards. In less than a second, the gate performs 64 checks on the magnetic encoding to ensure that the ticket is of correct value or zone, correct date and is still valid for further travel. If valid, the ticket coding is updated and the ticket returned. Once the ticket has been taken by the passenger, the gate paddles open. If the ticket is being checked at exit, it is retained when no longer valid.

Both the gates and the ticket issuing machines contain a Logic Control Processor which controls the overall operation, records transactions or basic statistical details and communicates with the station computer and thereby the central processors.

LUL operates two generations of ticket gate. The first uses air (from the signal air mains) to activate the paddle movements. There are three basic gate types: entry, exit and reversible. The reversible gate has four paddles and the others two.

The second generation gate is fully electric and uses an electric motor to move the paddles. There is only a reversible version of this gate and this has two paddles thereby allowing breakthrough in both directions. The stanchions on these gates are narrower than on the first design, which can offer useful space-saving.

All ticket gates are linked into an 'emergency open' circuit which allows all gates to be opened in an emergency. Plungers to activate this facility are typically located in ticket offices and ticket hall areas.

At ungated stations, tickets are checked visually by staff.

Revenue

London Underground's traffic revenue in 1996/7 was 797.3 million. Roughly, Underground revenue is derived about one-third from ordinary fares and two-thirds from the various Travelcard products. However, ordinary ticket holders pay rather more for their journeys than the overall average of £1.04. On a typical weekday, journey patterns by the main ticket types are as follows (1994/5 estimates). The proportion of Period Travelcard use falls sharply at weekends, when it is replaced by the One Day Travelcard:

Use of various ticket types	Journeys/Day	%
Ordinary ticket holders	561,000	23
One Day Travelcard	1,209,000	50
Period Travelcard	547,000	23
Concessionary Permits	94,000	4
Total	2,411,000	100

The overwhelming importance of the Travelcard for London Underground and its customers is apparent. In comparison, LT Buses rely much more heavily on Concessionary Permit revenue from London Boroughs, while 'bus only' passes are also important.

As related, Travelcard is also accepted by National Railways operators and the DLR, and it is between all these groups that ticket revenue must be shared. Primarily because of the involvement of National Railways, Travelcard pricing is now capped by the Rail Regulator. The Regulator requires Travelcard fares to be capped at an average of the inflation rate for three years from January 1996 and at 1% below the Retail Price Index for the following four years. Such a condition imposes very real limitations on London Underground in attempts to raise the revenue yield to fund investment.

PRESTIGE

In 1990, LUL undertook trials of contactless smartcard technology at Victoria, St James's Park and Green Park. This involved use of the cards by staff and by customers. The trials proved the general acceptability and convenience of smartcards and the ability to integrate the facility within the existing system architecture.

Work then commenced on the development of requirements for the introduction of Stored Value Ticketing (SVT). Originally, this assumed the use of enhanced magnetic technology, but was widened to include the use of contactless smartcards for both SVT and existing period pass tickets. The provision of network-wide gating was also investigated as it was considered this provided the best basis for the successful introduction of SVT, as well as containing fraudulent travel.

The objective of PRESTIGE is to provide a ticketing and revenue service which helps LUL understand its customers better and upgrades the service offered. Specifically, PRESTIGE will:

■ provide data on entry and exit, how the ticket is used and data analysis; this will assist service planning to meet demand;

■ reduce the need for ticket purchase transactions and allow faster movements through the gates with contactless cards;

■ allow the use of other sales outlets;

■ facilitate changes to fare levels and structures and the ticket products, and allow the introduction of customer loyalty schemes.

The PRESTIGE project is being taken forward under the Private Finance Initiative, which was launched by the last Government in 1992 to attract private sector involvement in public sector projects.

Revenue Protection

Most ticket fraud is accounted for by ticketless travel, over-riding the destination paid for, tickets out of zone, use of child tickets by adults, and passes being transferred to third parties. Counterfeiting and the use of stolen passes is less prevalent.

Revenue protection is undertaken by teams of line-based inspectors responsible for roving ticket checking, investigations and the issue of penalty fares. Penalty fares were introduced in April 1994, with the objective of reducing ticketless travel. There is a £10 on-the-spot fine which anyone travelling without a ticket is obliged to pay.

Right: Few Fare machine (left) and Multi Fare machine (right), as installed at Hillingdon.

The inspectors work in teams and check tickets at stations or on trains. The better sight lines on rolling stock with end windows has given ticketless travellers advance warning; one response has been the increased use of plain clothes inspectors.

One important objective is to maximise the opportunity to buy tickets in the first place, whether by machine acceptance of various coin/note combinations, upgrading change giving, or making zone extension tickets available from machine. Attention has also concentrated on ticket touts, who 'collect' used tickets, particularly One Day Travelcards, and then resell them.

Visual checks can be supplemented by the use of Psion-type ticket readers, which can check that the ticket coding agrees with the date on the face of the ticket. Some fraud is amazingly amateur. Not many people would consider altering a ticket dated 31 March to 32 March, but it has been tried! These inspectors are also responsible for investigating more complex types of fraud and for prosecutions.

Train Maintenance

The overhaul, maintenance and cleaning of rolling stock is planned on the basis of specified time intervals, which vary with the type of stock. All trains undergo a nightly test of specified safety devices plus an inspection of cab and saloons for damage. All should receive a nightly sweep and dust of car interiors and cleaning of driving cab windows. The nightly work is undertaken in depots or at stabling points as appropriate, and all other work is undertaken at a main depot. Full interior and exterior cleaning cycles are generally around every four weeks.

In addition to planned maintenance work, depots also undertake casualty repair work. Casualties are defined as rolling stock failures in service, but also include failures which prevent rolling stock going into service and work arising from an examination which results in the stock being withheld longer than planned.

Most stock has a periodic examination at 14 days, which includes the inspection and replacement of consumable items such as brake blocks and shoegear. Use of a pit is required for a comprehensive underside inspection and system testing. Normal time taken is a few hours, so this can be completed at night or in the inter-peak period.

Next is a shed day at around 30 weeks, depending on rolling stock type, but this is being extended in new builds to annually. This is a comprehensive inspection of the train, the programming of which varies from line to line to suit operational needs.

A programme lift is where the car body is removed, so that its bogies can be comprehensively examined and the wheels returned as necessary. This is also an opportunity to remove traction motors for overhaul.

Overhauls at nine and 27 years and heavy major overhauls at 18 years or half life are comprehensive. These includes the removal of the traction control equipment cases, which are sent to Acton workshops. Brake cylinders also receive attention.

Traction motors are maintained at up to six yearly intervals, compressors every three or four years according to type, and alternators/generators every six years.

Other work may of course take place as required, whether to ensure continuing reliability of the stock concerned, or to meet more recent performance standards.

Train Refurbishment

Underground trains last a long time and there is not always a very happy relationship between longevity, capital costs, changes in technology, new fire safety requirements, changes in traffic patterns and public tastes.

This has led to the now largely completed programme of upgrading, which commenced in 1989 with the C stock and the 1967 tube stock. A key requirement is to produce a more attractive travelling environment, but this should not obscure the replacement of flammable materials, new secondary suspensions and modifications to bogie frames to improve ride quality (C stock), replacement of flexible grab handles with a pole system to encourage a more even distribution of standing passengers, and relocation of equipment to aid emergency detrainment (1973 tube stock).

New interior colour schemes and finishes have been devised and applied, while all refurbished train sets have been finished externally in Underground corporate livery. This involves the application of a two-pack isocyanate paint system, which meets fire standards and offers excellent protection against graffiti, weathering and chipping. Graffiti can be removed from the finished surface without leaving shadowing or staining. All the indications are that the visible side of the refurbishment programme has been very well received by London Underground's customers.

Such work does have its costs, in the sense of the non-availability of each train for perhaps six weeks while the work is being carried out, as well as in the straightforward financial sense. As a rule of thumb, though, refurbishment costs around one-sixth of the cost of a new train.

7

SUPPORTING ORGANISATIONS

Railway Inspectorate

Her Majesty's Railway Inspectorate (HMRI) is a division of the Health & Safety Executive. HMRI has a particular role in the Safety Case regulations and safety principles generally.

Safety Case

The Railway (Safety Case) Regulations 1994 now place a requirement on all 'operators'; London Underground is at the same time the infrastructure controller, train operator and station operator.

A safety case has two main purposes:

■ to give confidence that the operator has the ability, commitment and resources to properly assess and effectively control risks to the health and safety of staff and the general public; and
■ to provide a comprehensive working document against which it can be checked that the accepted risk control measures and safety management systems have been properly put into place and continue to operate in the way in which they are intended.

London Underground's safety case was accepted by HMRI in early 1996. Another Regulation concerns Safety Critical Work and the assessment of staff competence.

Principles

The Railway Safety Principles and Guidance are published in two parts. Part One sets out the top level safety principles and gives an indication of the factors which need to be taken into account. Part Two, in eight sections concerning different aspects of railway construction, expands that advice in some detail and provides examples of good practice.

Soon after the Railway Inspectorate was formed in 1840, it issued the first written advice on the standards of construction which were thought to be important to the safety of the railway. It outlined good practice and helped to produce consistency between different places and different railways. The last full update was published in 1950.

The aim is for the Inspectorate to ensure that, when giving approval to new works, plant and equipment, all intolerable risks have been eliminated and that all remaining risks have been reduced to be as low as reasonably practicable.

It should perhaps be stressed, though, that this advice applies only to new installations and not retrospectively. However, there may be occasions on which some consequential changes may be needed to existing works.

The principles, of which there are 33, are set out in seven sections. These are:

■ Principle 1:   Safety mission
■ Principles 2-9:   Infrastructure
■ Principles 10-16:   Stations and stabling areas
■ Principles 17-19:   Electric traction systems
■ Principles 20-22:   Railway control systems
■ Principle 23:   Level crossings
■ Principles 24-33:   Trains

All, except level crossings, affect London Underground. For example, Principle 9: 'Tunnels and other enclosed spaces should provide a safe environment for people and safe evacuation. This includes the consideration of tunnel lengths, clearances, service frequencies, ventilation, fire detection, lighting, aerodynamic effects, escape routes, flooding risk, traction power supply isolation and emergency services access.'

Others include Principle 11: 'Platforms should allow for the safe waiting of people, their boarding and alighting from trains', and Principle 17: 'An electric traction system should not present safety hazards to people.'

Many are interdependent between different parts of the railway, such as Principle 20 on signalling: 'The signalling system should provide for the safe routeing, spacing and control of trains.' Or Principle 32 in the section on trains: 'The train should be dimensionally compatible with the infrastructure.'

The further Part Two sections on tramways and on heritage railways were unpublished as at mid-1997.

London Regional Passengers Committee

The London Regional Passengers Committee (LRPC), which represents the interests of bus and rail users in London, is an independent statutory body established under the London Regional Transport Act 1984. Its rail remit covers London Underground, the Train Operating Companies which serve London, Railtrack and Eurostar operations in London.

The Committee is required to consider representations about any matters relating to bus and rail services in and about London. It makes representations, as appropriate, to London Transport, the Rail Regulator, Railtrack, the operators, the Government and the Central Rail Users' Consultative Committee. The LRPC has a further duty to consider objections received to any proposal to withdraw passenger services totally from any railway station or section of line, and to report on any hardship which would result.

Railtrack

London Underground is remarkably self-contained, but there are sections of line where trains of a Train Operating Company also run on the same tracks (as north of Queen's Park on the Bakerloo) or use adjacent tracks in the same station (as at Upminster, District).

In both cases, management responsibility has to rest with one organisation, and financial adjustments made as necessary. The principal interfaces are as follows:

Sections of line owned by London Underground over which National Railways operators have running agreements:

Harrow-on-the-Hill-Amersham
East Putney-Wimbledon

Sections of line owned by Railtrack over which London Underground has a running agreement:

Gunnersbury-Richmond
Wimbledon station
Queen's Park-Harrow & Wealdstone

Below: This remarkable notice is to be found at the gate leading to what remains of the platforms at Down Street Piccadilly Line station, closed to passengers since 1932. To the best of the author's knowledge, steam trains have not been sighted, either before or since, at this location.

London Underground owns and operates 245 stations, but serves 20 more. The following are owned by Railtrack and leased to a Train Operating Company:

Barking
Gunnersbury
Harlesden
Harrow & Wealdstone
Kensal Green
Kensington (Olympia)
Kenton
Kew Gardens
New Cross
New Cross Gate
North Wembley
Queen's Park
Richmond
South Kenton
Stonebridge Park
Stratford
Upminster
Wembley Central
Willesden Junction
Wimbledon

It might be added that each Underground station is also 'owned' by a specific line and notices to this effect may be found on all London Underground stations.

Below: Railtrack still owns the station and the platform tracks at Wimbledon, although the rest of the line was acquired by London Underground on 1 April 1994. C stock and D stock trains are occupying Platforms 2 and 1 respectively.

Bottom right: Aldwych station, being served by a single train which shuttled to and from Holborn, had only a 9min frequency. The timings of the ancient lift which served the station were arranged to meet the trains and connect into and out of them. Missing the lift meant serious measures had to be taken, hence the notice at the top of the stairs.

Above: The break between London Underground and Railtrack on the Richmond branch is identified by this break in traction supplies at Acton Lane Junction. Formerly, there was a link to the right from this point leading to the North London Line, in the South Acton direction. A D stock train for Upminster approaches as a train for Richmond disappears in the distance.

Customer Information

IN THE
INTEREST
OF
SAFETY
PLEASE
DO NOT
RUN
DOWN
THE STAIRS

8
RAILWAY EXTENSIONS

Plans for system extension have always been a feature of the Underground, whether conceived at 55 Broadway or amongst the many formal (and some less formal) bodies which have an interest in transport in London.

New construction may be advanced for several reasons, amongst which are:

- the provision of new links which are not presently available;
- to relieve overcrowding on existing services;
- to regenerate areas of the capital facing decline and unemployment, feed newly developing areas; and
- to provide quality public transport as an alternative to private transport.

The emphasis has perhaps changed over the last half century. A main objective of the Victoria Line was new links, in which it succeeded admirably, but the Jubilee Line to Charing Cross was more concerned with tackling overcrowding on the then Bakerloo. Until 1979, this had two busy branches feeding into one constrained central area core.

The planning argument was in the end decisive, in a political sense, for the route of the Jubilee Line Extension

being via the south bank of the Thames to reach Canary Wharf in Docklands. It is instructive to compare the present routeing with that advocated 20 years ago.

Docklands was still the objective, but Stratford was not seen as a possible terminal. Relieving British Rail's North Kent line was perhaps a higher priority. Fenchurch Street would have received an Underground service, and the interchange to the East London Line was to be at Wapping.

More recently, what might loosely be called the environmental argument has taken hold, with an enlarged Underground system expected to do anything from what is rather inelegantly called road decongestion to improving air quality.

Jubilee Line Extension

Linking West End with East End, the Jubilee Line Extension provides quality, high capacity transport to Docklands and brings the Underground to southeast London.

Uniquely, the Jubilee interchanges with every other Underground line, including the Waterloo & City. Beneficiaries include London Bridge commuters with a

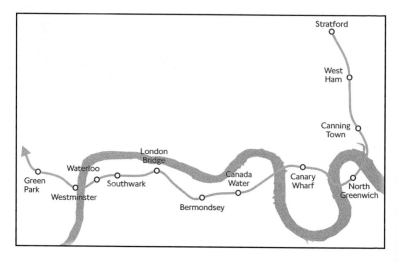

Above: Construction under way at Bermondsey JLE station in November 1995, showing the surface works.

Below right: A train of 1996 Jubilee Line stock stands in Ruislip depot with DM No 96019 at the front; a 1992 stock train is on the left of the picture.

link to Docklands and the West End, and those via both Stratford and Waterloo with a fast route to Canary Wharf.

The tunnelling started in London clay but then moved to the more difficult water-bearing sands and gravels from the Bermondsey area eastwards. There are four cross-river links: between Waterloo and Westminster; Canada Water and Canary Wharf; Canary Wharf and North Greenwich; and North Greenwich and Canning Town. The Underground is in an unparalleled position to provide such a linking together.

Construction is in deep level bored tube from Green Park to south of Canning Town, with cut-and-cover stations at Bermondsey, Canada Water, Canary Wharf and North Greenwich. The Extension has island platforms throughout except where space constraints dictate otherwise as at Westminster, with three platforms and a loop at North Greenwich to offer a terminating facility. There is judicious provision of crossovers between the tracks at other points.

The line returns to the surface at Canning Town, where it now parallels Railtrack's line to Stratford. The line

passes Stratford Market maintenance depot before reaching Stratford JLE station, which is a traditional Underground three platform arrangement.

Journey times are estimated as being 22min between Stratford and Green Park for the 11 stations (or 24min to Bond Street). This compares with 22min and 10 stations by Central Line from Stratford to Bond Street.

All stations except Bermondsey and North Greenwich have interchanges with other rail lines; that at Southwark is with the 'country' or eastern end of Waterloo East station.

Below: The Jubilee Line Extension from Stanmore extends the line via Waterloo to Stratford. A southbound 1983 stock train for Charing Cross arrives at Green Park, where the new line diverges from the 1979 construction. What further extensions north of Stratford might be contemplated?

Bottom: TA model of the platform edge doors and their mechanism, being installed at all new stations on the underground part of the Jubilee Line Extension. *Jubilee Line Extension Project*

Signalling and other equipment control systems are managed from a new Neasden Service Control Centre. A subsidiary control centre for train operating is located at Stratford Market for train movements within the depot and between the depot and the running lines.

Millennium Experience

London has from time to time been the home for major national exhibitions. These included the Great Exhibition of 1851, which with its 13,000 exhibits was designed to demonstrate to the world the technical progress and industrial supremacy of Britain. This was held in Hyde Park; the subsequent British Empire Exhibition (1924/5) was at Wembley and the Festival of Britain (1951) on the South Bank in the area of Waterloo symbolised postwar recovery.

All such events place substantial strains on the transport systems. The Millennium Experience at Greenwich is located on former industrial land at the north end of the Greenwich peninsula. London Underground's Jubilee Line Extension offers by far the most acceptable access route for many; North Greenwich station is strategically placed close to the entrance.

Ten million or more visitors are expected over the whole of the year 2000 during which the Millenium Experience is to be open. For those with a statistical mind, this is equivalent to the annual numbers of visitors to Madame Tussaud's, the Tower of London, the Natural History Museum, the Science Museum, London Zoo and St Paul's Cathedral all combined. The Underground is expected to carry more than half of the Millennium Experience visitors, so the scale of the transport requirements can be judged.

East London Line

The East London Line has suffered the indignity of extended closure and service replacement with buses. There are, however, ambitious plans for the line's extension. To the north, approval has been given under the Transport & Works Act procedures, though funding with an estimated requirement of about £80 million has yet to be found.

The 4km extension would run from north of Whitechapel with a new station at Bishopsgate to the west of, and replacing, the present Shoreditch station. The route then joins the southern end of the disused Broad Street railway viaduct and proceeds north along the viaduct with new stations at Hoxton and Haggerston. It would terminate initially at a station on the site of the former Dalston Junction BR.

A possible later extension over Railtrack's North London Line would allow the service to be extended via Canonbury to Highbury & Islington.

A new servicing facility would be constructed at Silwood, alongside the existing line south of Surrey Quays.

The southern extension, which has yet to be pursued, would leave the existing line south of Surrey Quays, running over former railway trackbeds. With one new intermediate station at Deptford Park, Railtrack property would be reached at the former Old Kent Junction, just north of Queen's Road, Peckham, station. The route would then continue over existing infrastructure via Peckham Rye to East Dulwich. The whole scheme is estimated to cost a further £30 million, making £110 million in all.

The service provision envisaged is as follows:

6tph	Highbury & Islington-Dalston Junction
12tph	Dalston Junction-Surrey Quays
4tph	Surrey Quays-New Cross
4tph	Surrey Quays-New Cross Gate
4tph	Surrey Quays-East Dulwich

Other factors for consideration include line capacity on the extensions over Railtrack, technical compatibility, the southern destination alternatives other than East Dulwich (of which several have been canvassed by local authority interests), and whether this is really an Underground project.

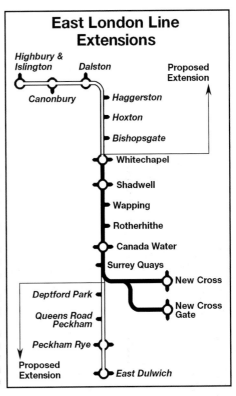

Above: **The East London Line extension proposals, both north and south of the present railway.**

Croxley Link

The Croxley link is a proposal to extend the Metropolitan Line train service via Croxley into Watford Junction, from its present site on the outskirts.

From the branch, the route would be via a new station at Ascot Road, with park-and-ride facilities for 200 cars, bus and taxi interchange, and cycle storage. The route would then proceed via the effectively defunct Railtrack Croxley Green single-track branch, with the existing station at Watford West. Joining the existing dc lines once used by the Bakerloo but nowadays the preserve only of North London Railways, Underground trains would proceed to

Watford High Street and Watford Junction. The present Watford (Met) station would be closed.

This would be achieved by the construction of a new 500m viaduct to bridge the A412 road, the River Gade and the Grand Union Canal. The cost of the scheme, which would include doubling the Railtrack branch, is put at £25 million.

Other additional station sites have been identified.

Below: **The Terminal 5 extension of the Piccadilly Line would run alongside the Heathrow Express Railway.**

Benefits for existing Underground users from Harrow and Pinner include destinations much more useful to visitors to Watford than the present 1925 terminus, for which the problems of a route through Cassiobury Park to the town centre proved insurmountable. Besides giving access to Virgin Trains at Watford Junction, Watford is a regional commercial centre and High Street station is well situated.

Watford itself gains access to the Underground network, while the possibility exists of direct services between Amersham, Rickmansworth and Watford Junction via the existing but little used Watford North curve. But this has far more potential than just an Underground link. Chiltern Trains could use it for an

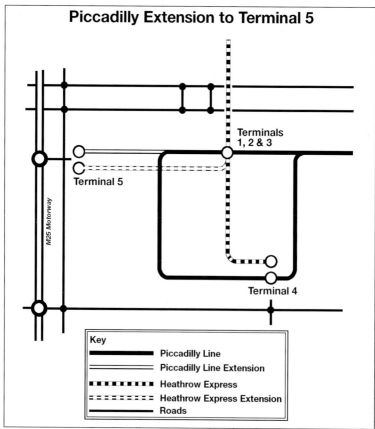

Piccadilly Extension to Terminal 5

Terminals 1, 2 & 3

Terminal 5

M25 Motorway

Terminal 4

Key

▬▬▬▬ Piccadilly Line
═══════ Piccadilly Line Extension
■■■■■■■■ Heathrow Express
= = = = = = Heathrow Express Extension
▬▬▬▬ Roads

Aylesbury-Watford Junction service, or if ways could be found of making a quick dart across the fast lines, Marylebone to St Albans City. All the options require access over sections of line which are presently under two different owners, but where will funding for the link come from and with what strings attached?

London Underground expects to submit a Transport & Works Act application for powers to build the link.

Terminal 5

If Heathrow Terminal 5 is built, there is a strong chance that the Piccadilly Line will be extended to it.

There are a number of areas of difficulty here. First, how does one plan to run a sensible service, given that T5 will be beyond the central terminal area, and T4 on its present loop will be out on a limb?

A statement by LUL and BAA says that the extension would run in tunnels from west of the central terminal area, with the westbound tunnel passing under the T4 loop. There would be a sub-surface station at T5, alongside that of the Heathrow Express Railway. 'All trains would serve the central terminal area and there would be separate services to T4 and T5.'

This could be read to imply that T4 would become a single-track stub served via the CTA and the Hatton Cross-T4 section abandoned, giving a service pattern

analogous to an underground Finchley Central (!), but this need not be the case. Some trains could continue to run as at present, or shuttles could be contemplated. Most alternatives have their problems in terms of passenger confusion, operational difficulties such as lack of recovery time, or enhanced infrastructure provision.

Second, by definition, Piccadilly trains which go to Heathrow do not go to Rayners Lane/Uxbridge. If Heathrow traffic continues to grow — and there is little point in building T5 if it does not — how are the two destinations to be balanced?

Lastly, what does the Underground need to do to compete as effectively as it is able with the Heathrow Express Railway?

The Piccadilly extension to T5 is costed at £70 million.

CrossRail

The CrossRail concept is to link suburban operations by National Railways to the east and west of London by a new deep level bored tunnel through the centre. Specifically, the Great Eastern local services from Shenfield into Liverpool Street would be diverted in tunnel to a combined Liverpool St/Moorgate underground station, thence to Farringdon, Tottenham Court Road, Bond Street and Paddington. Out on the GW main line, services would proceed to Reading or to Aylesbury (plus the Chesham branch) via a new connection in the

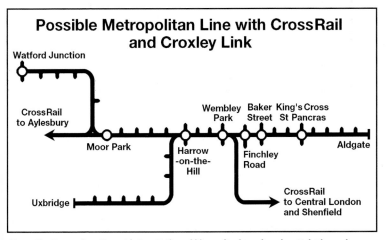

Above: **The Metropolitan Line with CrossRail would be confined to a branch to Uxbridge and a branch to Watford, but one might speculate that the latter will by then be rerouted to Watford.**

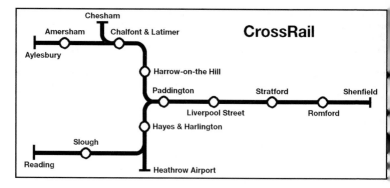

Above: The CrossRail scheme as planned from Shenfield to Aylesbury and Reading, with branches to serve Chesham and Heathrow Airport.

Old Oak Common area to the Dudding Hill line and Neasden. Another possible destination in the west is Heathrow.

The involvement of London Underground derives in part from the construction of what would have become, effectively, additional platforms at central London stations already owned and managed by London Underground. The operator (or operators) whose trains happen to use those platforms could be considered a side issue. However, in northwest London, CrossRail would effectively take over services presently operated by the Metropolitan Line. The result would be that the Metropolitan Line would run to Uxbridge and to Watford (Metropolitan), or perhaps Watford Junction, only. Operations by the Underground to Rickmansworth and beyond would cease. There are also issues of dual-voltage stock or system conversion, given that the Great Eastern and most of the Great Western lines are electrified at 25kV ac, and the Underground section at 630V dc fourth rail. Other sections, including that beyond Amersham, are presently not electrified at all.

Use of CrossRail would avoid much interchange by passengers to the present Underground system, since City as well as West End destinations would be available. The projected capital cost was not modest. Everything about the CrossRail scheme was large scale. Eight-car trains with 23m vehicles running at 24tph need platforms of 190m and can carry 26,400 passengers per single hour. (The scheme would allow for future expansion to 12-coach trains at 36tph with 285m

platforms.) Purpose-built underground stations to cope with these numbers take up a lot of room. The construction bill was put at £2.85 billion.

CrossRail, for so long in the 'nearly authorised' category, fell by the wayside when the enabling Bill failed to pass the scrutiny of the Private Bill Committee in 1994. The reasons were not given, but it is fair to say that the MPs on the Committee were not convinced of the merits of the case put to them.

Was CrossRail the right scheme? Central Line traffics have always shown a decided imbalance between the numbers originating in the east of London and in the

Below: The Chelsea-Hackney Line would take over the Central Line's Epping branch northwards from Leytonstone. The burrowing junction where the Hainault loop diverges is seen here in 1990, with a southbound 1962 stock train emerging from the tunnel section. The latter is very obviously tube gauge only, while the rest looks like real railway.

west. Similarly, even suburban traffic into Marylebone and Paddington combined, also allowing for that on the Metropolitan, is hard put to match that on the 'electric lines' into Liverpool Street. But even in the east, there is a newly and expensively modernised Central Line to help take the load; do we really need a third railway between Stratford and Bond Street? As a senior planner remarked to the author, 'Virtually nothing in the entire scheme is financially justified. I suppose that running trains if somebody has actually built the tunnel might be.'

There are other opportunities for new links, where present journeys are less than straightforward. The Tilbury line into Fenchurch Street offers a less than attractive destination for those wanting the West End, while access to the CrossRail route from the West Coast main line in the Kensal Green area would also bring new benefits.

CrossRail, your flexible friend, links Milton Keynes and Southend?

The existing CrossRail route remains formally safeguarded. If resurrected, the priority of the former Conservative government was that it should precede the Chelsea-Hackney Line.

Chelsea-Hackney

This scheme was proposed in 1991 by London Underground as a means of relieving central London congestion and linking the southwest and northeast suburbs.

The objectives were:

■ to increase the capacity of Central London's rail system;

■ to serve new areas of London such as King's Road Chelsea, Dalston and Hackney;

■ to provide congestion relief on overcrowded sections of the Underground, particularly the Victoria Line in the central area;

■ to offer a significant reduction in journey times to areas poorly served by rail; and

■ to provide increased dispersal capacity at King's Cross, St Pancras and Victoria.

The last has particular relevance to the additional traffic which will result from the Channel Tunnel Rail Link terminal construction at St Pancras.

The Chelsea-Hackney Line would provide a service from Wimbledon to Epping, utilising the existing District Line between Wimbledon and Parsons Green, and the Central Line between Leytonstone and Epping.

Parsons Green and Leytonstone would be linked by a new 18.8km tunnel through central London. Intermediate stations would all be interchange points with other lines (Underground and/or National Railways), with a completely new station location at King's Road Chelsea.

This tube gauge route has been safeguarded.

Later thoughts have suggested a number of alternatives. With the South-West to North-East Metro cachet, alternatives canvassed were three different possibilities for linking Victoria and East Putney, the deletion of central area stations at Sloane Square, Piccadilly Circus and Angel, and the substitution of Highbury & Islington for Essex Road. Beyond Hackney Central, a route via Railtrack's North London Line to Stratford was an alternative to Epping.

The result was a reduction of the £2.4-£2.8 billion capital cost to around one half, depending on the option chosen; the length in tunnel is between 10km and 11km in all the Metro alternatives. An important difference is that the Metro would be constructed to full Railtrack loading gauge, which might offer a whole host of new

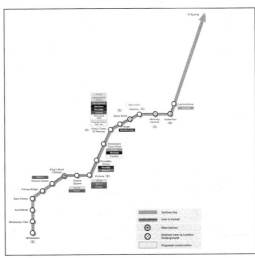

***Right:** The Chelsea-Hackney safeguarded route.*

Above: **If the Chelsea-Hackney Line were to be progressed, trains on the Wimbledon branch of the District would not need to proceed beyond Parsons Green. A D stock train approaches Fulham Broadway, opened in 1880, albeit that the station was then named Walham Green.**

with A stock) and others.

The searching out of new links where none existed previously is a far more attractive alternative.

The second problem is that of National Railways lines which disgorge their passengers onto an Underground network for journeys within Zone 1 at points where it is perhaps least able to accept them. The CrossRail approach is probably the right way to overcome an historical problem, provided capital costs can be kept within bounds. From the point of view of the Underground, such passengers pay relatively little in the way of fares when their Travelcard revenue is apportioned.

possibilities. In this connection, it is perhaps helpful to remember that Leytonstone-Epping and East Putney-Wimbledon were owned formerly by the Great Eastern and London & South Western Railways respectively.

No decision on the relative merits of the various options has been reached.

The schemes might lop about 7min off the Central Line Tottenham Court Road to Epping times, but even 40min sounds a long time to a destination 30km distant. Wimbledon seems to fare better, at 20min. Here, a present-day journey by Northern Line to Waterloo thence South West Trains takes 20min running time plus interchange and waiting time. The distance is about 15km, so the average speed of the South West to North East Metro is much the same in each case. Is it possible to do better?

This approach leads to a consideration of the respective roles of national railway operators vis-à-vis London Underground. Who should determine what services should be provided under the Passenger Services Requirement, and with what objective in mind?

That is perhaps the crux of the matter. Is the role of the Underground and other public transport providers in London to run an integrated service for the benefit of the community, or to maximise profits? Either way, what is the role of the private sector, whether in the development of infrastructure or in the operation of services?

Tomorrow's System

It has always seemed undesirable to duplicate existing provision merely to relieve overcrowding, unless there really is no reasonable alternative. Line capacity is not fixed and can be increased by a variety of measures. These include a more frequent service with the aid of more moving block signalling (Jubilee Line), platform extension to run longer trains (Central Line, 1930s), altering the door/seat ratios of rolling stock to increase standing capacity (C stock compared

Below: **The crossing of the Grand Union Canal by a Watford-Baker Street train of A stock in April 1977 shows the train to be depressingly empty.**

9

A 21st CENTURY SYSTEM

London's economy is very substantial, to the extent that it accounts for nearly a fifth of the UK Gross Domestic Product. If London catches a cold, the whole country does so, and so do London's transport providers.

The transport industry is rarely in charge of its destiny, since transport is not a good which is often purchased out of choice. Rather, people need to get to their place of employment and choose their means accordingly. That may result in journeys by London Underground, and if people's employment is in central London, there is a high chance that they will use rail to get there. London Underground and National Railways are together responsible for three-quarters of central London commuting.

As has been shown earlier, for London Underground, serving the commuter market to central London is a basic business. LUL carries 600,000 to work and back every day; these are 70% in social groups ABC1, while 70% are under 35. There is at least an argument that the product is underpriced.

What do we need to do with the Underground so that it can be every bit as successful in the future as it has been over the last 130 or so years? The Decently Modern Metro product was a very simple idea, offering a value for money railway which would be safe, clean, quick, reliable and efficient. For the train service to offer this, it needs a well-maintained and updated infrastructure to support it. This is not too much for Londoners to expect from their Underground system.

As a result, London employers improve their competitiveness, while reduced congestion raises the supply of labour and gives a supply side boost to the London economy. Government tax revenues increase from a boost to economic activity and the reduction in benefit payments.

Let us try a strengths, weaknesses, opportunities and threats, or SWOT, analysis for London Underground. These are suggested as follows, in no particular order within their groups:

Strengths
■ Acknowledgment that the Underground must provide what its customers want.
■ As brands, 'Underground' and 'London Transport'

Above: A refurbished A stock train from Aldwych leaves Baker Street for the City. Might this be the most productive place for London Underground to seek future capital investment monies?

are exceedingly well known, throughout Britain and to the incoming business and tourist trades from overseas.

■ Unit production costs per train km have fallen by 15% in real terms since 1990/1.

■ Service levels are generally high and planned to increase further.

■ The Underground's customer satisfaction ratings have improved substantially in recent years.

■ The service provided is relatively inexpensive for the passenger.

■ Travel by Underground is socially acceptable, as evidenced by the social class distribution of its customers.

Weaknesses

■ The Underground is little used for short journeys, nor is it very suitable.

■ The system is once again underfunded for core infrastructure renewals, an area in which there is a substantial backlog, and there is little stability over time in that level of funding.

■ An inability to respond quickly to changes in demand patterns, given that the infrastructure is 'fixed' in most senses.

■ Accessibility to the Underground is poor for the less physically able.

■ Capital costs of system extensions are very high.

■ Any tendency to over-engineer project specifications, which makes them unjustifiable from a business point of view.

■ The Underground is a slow means of travel for long distances to Zone 5 and Zone 6 suburbs, in terms of journey time.

Opportunities

■ The Private Finance Initiative may be a means of unlocking capital funds and converting them to payments from the revenue budget.

■ Road pricing, depending upon how it might be applied, plus growing concern about the environment, may make the Underground a more attractive travel option.

■ Joint ventures with Railtrack and/or Train Operating Companies may offer new and profitable service opportunities.

■ There may be scope for thinning out the network through closing some little used stations, particularly if closely spaced, as was undertaken on the Piccadilly Line in the early 1930s.

■ Property and commercial trading development at particularly well placed stations, as practised by Railtrack

at its independently managed stations.

■ Making the best use of what we have: the scope for a reorientation of service patterns, mainly on the surface lines, to link new origins and destinations at minimal expense.

Threats

■ The general irrelevance of Underground services for most journeys in the outer suburbs, particularly non-radial ones.

■ An inability to match future demand growth, particularly if the infrastructure is unable to accommodate higher levels of service provision.

■ Out-of-town shopping or commercial developments, and lower density housing, which cannot be served effectively by Underground.

Private Finance Initiative

This concept is worth describing in some detail in respect of the supply of new 1995 stock trains for the Northern Line by GEC-Alsthom.

This was the first major use of the Private Finance Initiative for a large-scale transport project, an arrangement which requires the public sector beneficiary to demonstrate to the Treasury that a significant amount of risk has been transferred to the private sector. The concept adopted in this case is that of train service availability, rather than rolling stock leasing. The contract is for 20 years, with options to extend; the trains remain throughout in the ownership of GEC-Alsthom.

GEC-Alsthom takes on full responsibility for the design, manufacture, maintenance and cleaning of both trains and trackside equipment. London Underground's requirement is for a guaranteed 96 trains for peak service being made available and then running reliably whilst in service. Consequently, the supplier takes the onus for the management and re-equipment of the rolling stock depots. Train radio and CCTV are also down to GEC-Alsthom. The former London Underground staff at Morden and Golders Green depots are now employed by GEC-Alsthom.

LUL, on the other hand, is committed to the maintenance of a specified environment and track standards to enable the supplier to plan with some certainty. The PFI deal has had to be complemented with capital expenditure by LUL of nearly £120 million over three years, completing in 1997. This has been necessary to bring the Northern Line tunnel clearances, power supplies and track up to a basic standard (Phase 1), though the subsequent stages of resignalling

(Phase 2) and comprehensive infrastructure upgrading (Phase 3) are needed to maximise the benefit from the new trains. These latter phases are victims of the Chancellor's 1996 statement and have been postponed.

The contract transfers the following risks to GEC-Alsthom:

■ Design and Construction risk. GEC-Alsthom carries the risk for the design, manufacture and delivery of the trains and equipment, though LUL continues to bear the risk of maintaining a specified environment such as track standards and tunnel profile.
■ Service Availability. GEC-Alsthom is responsible for specifying the number of trains (including the number of spares) against a maximum specified service requirement.
■ Performance Risk. GEC-Alsthom carries the risk for the performance and reliability of the trains throughout the 20 year primary usage period. LUL has an option to extend into a secondary period on the same basis.

■ Residual Value Risk. LUL is committed only to procure a service for 20 years, representing a significant residual risk to the supplier.
■ Early Termination. GEC-Alsthom must achieve a pre-agreed performance and reliability target substantially better than the present best on the Underground, or LUL can exit the contract.

The key is that the responsibility for maintaining the trains and supplying them daily to the operator in the numbers required, in a satisfactory condition, is that of GEC-Alsthom. The payments by LUL of £40-£45 million a year are performance related, and if GEC-Alsthom fails to provide enough trains in full working order, payments are reduced. The deductions will also be weighted according to the time of day and the location on the line where the failure occurred.

Revenue risk remains primarily with London Underground, but the contract gives it the option of introducing a risk sharing arrangement with the supplier.

Below: **Morden depot with trains of 1959 stock and a solitary 1972 MkI stock train, while a little gentle track maintenance is under way. This is now the responsibility of GEC-Alsthom through its subsidiary company Railway Maintenance Services Ltd.**

In London Underground's view, the costs of completing such deals are significant, and the contracts impose substantial future liabilities. Projects are complex and take up to two years to reach agreement from the time of inception. PFI may not be appropriate for all capital investment needs, while achieving value for money is heavily dependent on the successful transfer of risk to the private sector.

Other deals which may be struck under the Private Finance Initiative include PRESTIGE (ticketing), Power supplies, Connect (integrated radio service), Piccadilly to T5, East London Line extension(s), the Croxley link, escalators, Phases 2 and 3 of the Northern Line infrastructure project, refurbished trains for the District Line, new trains for Victoria Line, Wembley Park station reconstruction and track modernisation.

Business Rate

There are of course other ways of raising capital for transport infrastructure investment in London, if the Government of the day is unwilling or unable to contribute directly. One is through taxation on employers. Businesses would be consulted on the levy, both in terms of what it would be designed to achieve (which indirectly determines the amount required) and how it would be applied. Thus, the use of resources would be determined by those who paid. Levy payers would have to give assent, a package of projects would be offered and a vote would take place. Funding would have to be determined in advance; some capital projects would need to be secure for five or more years, but other

funding could be determined on an annual or biannual basis.

Each levy payer would be entitled to vote. The number of votes might be in direct proportion to the rateable value of business properties, or banded. Votes would be cast by the Company Secretary.

A body would be needed to administer this and take responsibility for setting and using the levy.

Such ideas are not entirely fanciful; an existing scheme is that of the French 'verse transports'.

The Government's Plans for London

'Legislation will be introduced to provide for a referendum on a directly elected strategic authority and a directly elected mayor for London'. Thus, Her Majesty the Queen stated at the State Opening of Parliament on 14 May 1997. This will be the first time that such an authority has existed since the abolition of the Greater London Council in 1986, and would re-establish London on the same international footing as other major world cities, such as New York, Paris or Barcelona.

Below: **Mornington Crescent station, one of the finer remaining 'ox-blood' stations, was closed for rebuilding in 1992. A major factor was the condition of the lifts, which were the originals dating from the station's opening in 1907. Services will be resumed in 1997.**

Legislation in 1998 would pave the way for elections in May 2000 and a 2001 start. The Greater London Authority (GLA) is to take overall responsibility for issues with a London-wide dimension, such as economic regeneration, planning, policing, environmental protection and, of course, transport. A subsidiary London Transport Authority, appointed by the GLA, would have responsibility for bus and tube services and assume oversight of roads strategic to London. The LTA would become the successor to London Regional Transport, a corporation presently responsible to the Secretary of State. As we have seen, the status of London Transport and its successors has changed over the years, oscillating between national and local authority masters.

A related question is the arrangements to be made for National Railways, or at least the 10 companies which were formerly part of Network SouthEast whose services enter London. The 1977 Green Paper 'New Leadership for London' suggested that responsibility should remain with central Government, but the LTA would need to be able to influence decisions made on rail services, management and investment in London.

Overall, the GLA 'will produce a transport strategy which delivers a clean, efficient, safe and reliable transport system, consistent with national transport and planning policies and strategies for air quality, noise and helping to control emissions of greenhouse gases. It will cover all forms of transport, dealing with London's national and international links as well as journeys in and around London'.

Perhaps a newly-elected Government, which has supportive views towards public transport and the environment, is the greatest opportunity of all for London Underground.

Above: This is a 1987 poster, 'Take Off' by Wilson McLean, commissioned by London Underground. Whatever attributes the Piccadilly Line may have, one would not consider it supersonic, but then neither are the fares.

Below: The sad external state to which much Underground rolling stock descended is demonstrated in this view of C stock units at Paddington Praed Street station.

Above: Watford Junction saw Bakerloo Line trains for 65 years, but they disappeared finally in 1982. A 1938 stock train arrives on a rainy morning on 20 April 1977, destination indicator already changed for the next journey. Again, the different floor heights of tube and, in this case, Class 501 units, are noticeable.

Leaves you breathless.
Rather like the air in London.

Above: Advertising is not necessarily kind to the local area in which it appears. This is one of a series of advertisements promoting Scotland for holidays and appeared in 1996.